THE BOOK OF
OTTERY ST MARY
with West Hill & Escot

THE BOOK OF
OTTERY ST MARY

with West Hill & Escot

The Birthplace of Samuel Taylor Coleridge

GERALD GOSLING AND PETER HARRIS

HALSGROVE

First published in Great Britain in 2004

Copyright © 2004 Gerald Gosling and Peter Harris

This book is dedicated to the people of Ottery St Mary, past, present and future.

British Library Cataloguing-in-Publication Data.
A CIP record for this title is available from the British Library.

ISBN 1 84114 333 2

HALSGROVE

Halsgrove House
Lower Moor Way
Tiverton, Devon EX16 6SS
Tel: 01884 243242
Fax: 01884 243325
E-mail: sales@halsgrove.com
Website: www.halsgrove.com

Title page: *Ottery St Mary from St Mary's Church, c.1980.*

Printed and bound in Great Britain by CPI Bath.

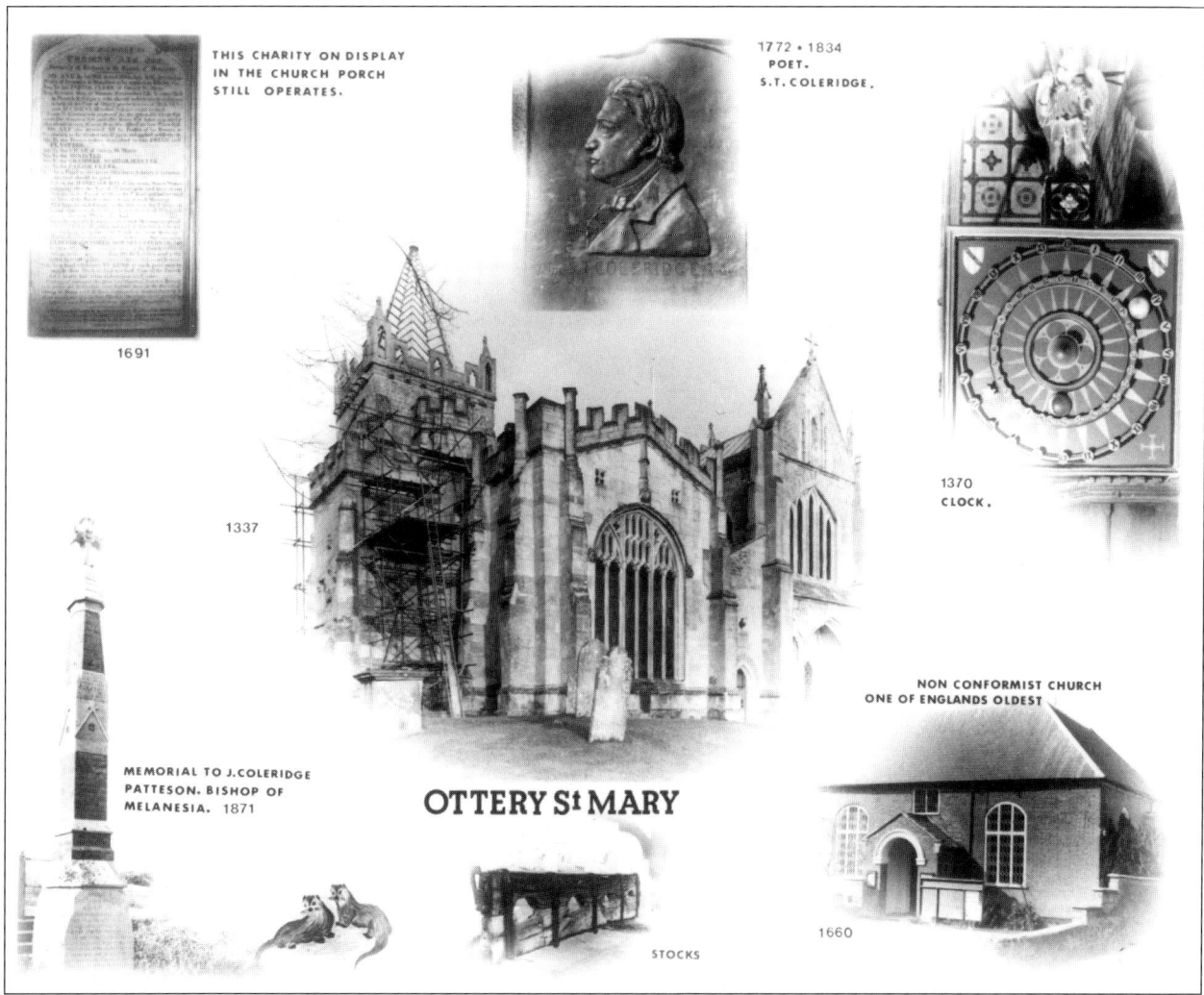

THIS CHARITY ON DISPLAY
IN THE CHURCH PORCH
STILL OPERATES.

1691

1772 • 1834
POET.
S.T. COLERIDGE.

1370
CLOCK.

1337

MEMORIAL TO J.COLERIDGE
PATTESON. BISHOP OF
MELANESIA. 1871

OTTERY St MARY

STOCKS

NON CONFORMIST CHURCH
ONE OF ENGLANDS OLDEST

1660

An Ottery St Mary montage by Keith Bowden.

Acknowledgements

We are more than grateful to those who have allowed us to include their pictures, memorabilia or memories in this book and must thank them all: Ottery St Mary Library, *Pulman's Weekly News*, the *Western Gazette*, the late Fred Baker, Ray Baker, Frank Bastin, Jenny Bess (née Carter), Peter Blanchard, Keith Bowden, Pat Harris, Ron Homer, John Lovell, Jim Isaac, Mollie Nancekivell, Ottery St Mary Cricket Club, Jim and Rosemary Pearcy, John Pilsworth, Marjorie Rix (née Paddon), Peter and Val Venner, Malcolm and Marion White.

The carillon in the tower at St Mary's Church that plays the Ottery Song.

THE OTTERY SONG

There is a place, dear native place!
Amid the meadows fair,
Between the hills, beside the stream,
Where blows the soft light air.

Chorus: O! Ottery dear, O! Ottery fair!
My heart goes out to thee,
Thou art my home, where'er I roam
The West! The West for me.

Sweet-breathing kine, the old grey church,
The curfew tolling slow
The glory of the Western sky,
The warm red earth below
Chorus: O! Ottery dear...

The whistling Cock, the tumbling weir,
The cave where Pixies dwell
The sweet old place which gave us birth
We know – we love it well.
Chorus: O! Ottery dear...

Then let us clap each other's hands,
Our Childhood's love renew,
We stand together round the World,
For Ottery Hearts are true.
Chorus: O! Ottery dear...

Bernard, Lord Coleridge, 1910

CONTENTS

St Mary's Church, seen from the grounds of the Marist Convent in the 1950s.

Chapter 1

General History

The Making of State and Shire

Over the graves of the Druids and under the wreck of Rome,
Rudely but surely they bedded the plinth of the days to come.
Behind the feet of the legions and before the Norseman's ire
Rudely but greatly begat they the framing of state and state.
Rudely but deeply they laboured and their labour stands till now,
If we trace on our ancient headlands the twist of their eight-ox plough.

No one could put it better than Rudyard Kipling does in one of his best poems, *The King's Task*. Our Saxon forbears, a likeable and intelligent race from whom the English get almost all of their better qualities, indeed left their visible traces on our ancient headlands and almost everywhere else as well.

The Romans certainly built many good roads, but their mileage pales into insignificance compared to that of the Saxons who arrived in England some 90 years after the departure of the Romans in AD410. Where two landowners' property met each would more than likely erect a hedge and it was between

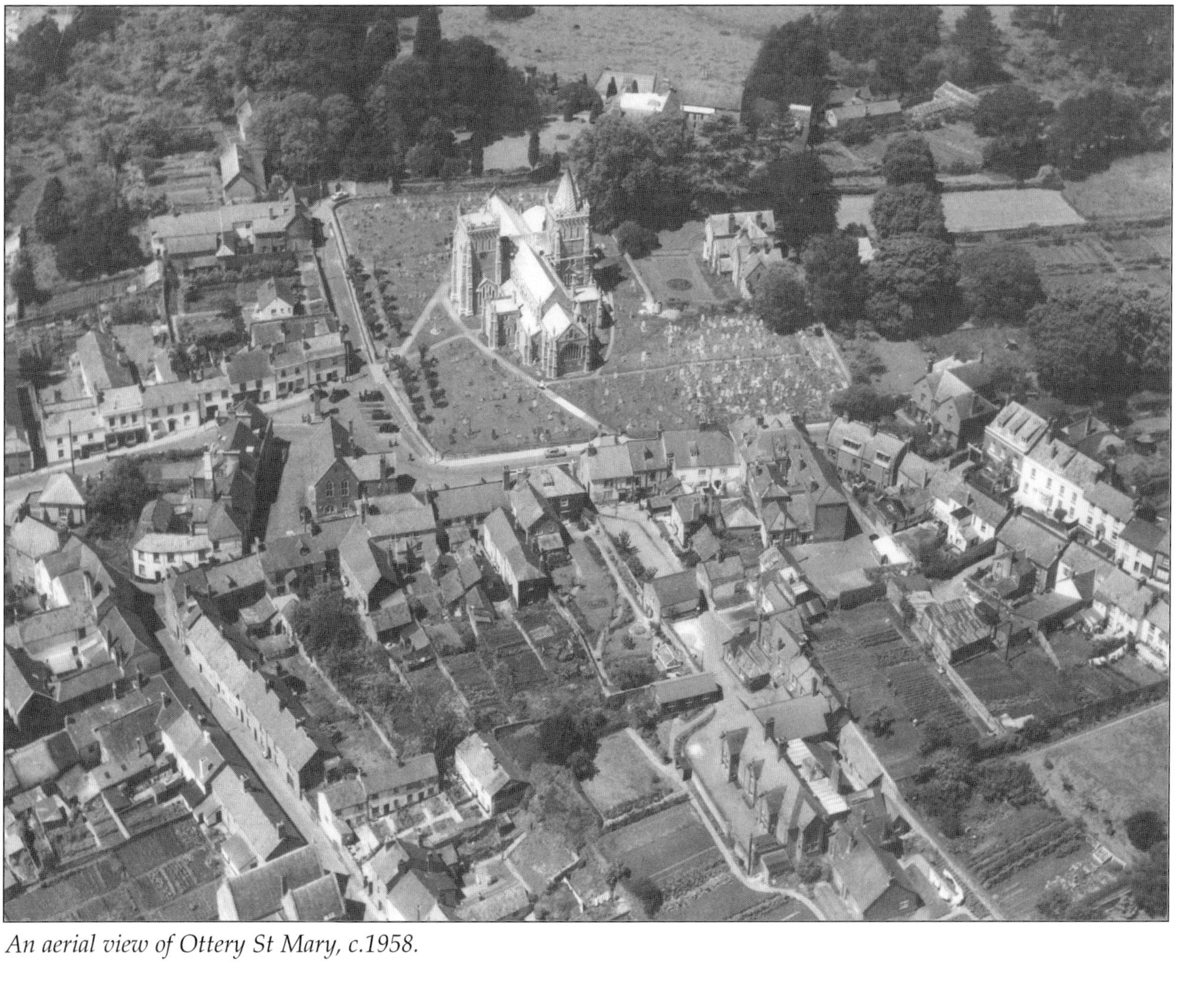

An aerial view of Ottery St Mary, c.1958.

many of these double hedges that people walked. In time they became public paths and then lanes and roads. This is the reason why today in many parts of Devon you will suddenly come across a lane that starts and ends without a reason. They are parts of ancient Saxon roads that have survived a later removal of portions of those 'lanes' in the interests of increasing the size of a field.

Several neighbouring fields were shaped to give each one access to a pond or a stream – a reason for the often bewildering twisting and turnings of our hedges. Or a hedge was planned to include a large boulder or tree stump rather than face the labour necessary to remove them when woodlands were being cleared. This in turn also gave way to 'the rolling English drunkard and his rolling English road.'

But we also owe almost all of our cities, towns and villages, and most of our farms, to the Saxons as well. As the forests were cleared, settlements grew up in places where there were both water and workable land. Some stayed on as farms, others, depending on their economical position (coal, tin, timber, etc.) or strategic position (by an important river crossing or a natural harbour), grew in size. There are few settlements in England that were not there by the time of Hastings, fewer still by the time of Agincourt in 1415. In modern times there have been a few purpose-built towns – Bournemouth, for instance, appeared from almost nowhere in the early-nineteenth century. The rest? Even their names have been corrupted down the centuries from their Old and Middle English origins. And it was those Saxons that left the traces of their labours all over Ottery. Just how important they considered the town can best be gauged from the fact they made it a hundred in its own right and, unusually so, it was the only place in its hundred. A hundred was a subdivision of a shire and the term persisted until it was abolished by the County Court Act of 1867.

Indeed the boundary of the modern parish is much the same as it was in the eleventh century, when an ancient charter mapped out the boundaries of the then small settlement. The charter takes us from 'straetgeat', today's Straightway Head, on the old A30 above Fairmile, to 'taleford'. It crosses the River Tale close to the present Taleford, thence up the Tale to the 'blind spring', presumably the point where the present boundary leaves the Tale and makes a dogleg bend eastwards. Thence to 'dene beorg', which is the barrow beside the railway which gives the name to some fields called Denbury, then to 'haeofeld mere', a name that is with us today as Heathfield Brake, a nearby field, then to 'finan', Vine Water, and then to 'Otrig' (the River Otter). Almost certainly there have been some slight changes in the boundaries at this point, Vine Water being outside the parish. From the Otter the boundary runs on to 'straetford', most likely the place where the old Roman road fords the river, and from there to the middle of 'eromdun', most

likely Gittisham Hill. From there the old boundary follows the 'hollow way', the 'red flood' and southwards along the down to the 'wyrtrum' as far as 'wicgincland' (Wiggaton). At this point the present boundary runs along Landscore Lane to Westgate Hill and then follows the old Ridgeway that continues south past Wiggaton. The boundary then carries on to 'waecces treow' (Waxway Farm that is just to the west of the present boundary near Tipton St John), the tree ('treow') having been replaced as the boundary marker by the present white cross. The next point is 'berrdescumbes heafod' (Hollow Head Cross that gives its name to Burscombe in Sidbury). Then the boundary runs to 'leofan dune', the present Beacon Hill, and on to 'cetes holt' (still recorded in 1612 as 'chettisholt' and today known as Harpford Woods). The line runs down to the Otter, which it meets at the 'borstenan clifie' and from there to the 'pinfold' and to the southern 'ellem ford'. Today's boundary crosses the Otter and twists towards the 'hricweg', probably the ridge road that goes past Metcombe. The charter takes the boundary past several places that are not recognisable today; 'apolder true', 'stanford' (Old English for Lower Ford) and 'raegen dornas'. From 'raegen dornas' the boundary runs north to 'hearpad'. Here we are on the Roman road at Tipton Cross. Hearpad, 'the warriors' way', can be found at Seaton as 'herpo', today's Harepath Hill, which was, of course, part of that same Roman road. The last stretch takes us along 'hearpad' back to 'straetgeat'.

Ottery St Mary appears in many forms from those times. In 1061 we have 'Otrig land', 'Otri' in the Domesday Book (1086) and 'Sca Maria de Otery' in 1207. Others include 'Otery Sancte Marie', 'Ottreg St Mary' and 'Austrey St Mary', the latter appearing as recently as 1675.

Among farms and places in Ottery St Mary that are identifiable today are Belbury Castle, in lower Broadoak Road, West Hill. There is a reference in 1061 to 'bigulfesburh'. The 'burh' refers to an old earthwork and can be found as '-bury' all around Ottery St Mary, as in Musbury, Blackbury Castle, Membury, Hembury Fort, Sidbury, Woodbury and many others.

'Cadhay' is found as 'cadehegh' in 1238 and later as 'cadheye' and 'cadheie'. In 1249 it was the home of William Cadey.

'Cheyneway' and 'chyneway' have been corrupted into today's Chineway and could take its name from 'chine' (spine or backbone). The road goes across the ridge of East Hill, hence the spine.

Many place names originate from a previous owner. Knightstone Farm was the home of the le Knight family in 1275, Salston House (today Salston Hotel) was Salveston in 1243 and was the home of the family of Jordan Saluin. Wiggaton is older and can be found as Wygeton in 1289. It is a corruption of the Old English (Saxon) 'Wiga's farm' or 'land'.

Ottery's Story
By Ron Homer

The Saxons invaded East Devon in the seventh century following their victory at the Battle of Beandun in 614, said by some to have been fought at Bindon near Axmouth. The Saxons built settlements as they went and among their early ones would have been Axminster, Colyton, Sidbury and Woodbury. By around 700 it is at least likely that a nucleated settlement was established at Ottery. That Ottery was a place of some significance by the tenth century is attested by the fact that it was a hundred in its own right.

A hundred was a Saxon administrative unit that had as an essential feature its own court of law. It also had certain financial and military obligations to the Crown. There were several small settlements around Ottery, some of which – Tipton, Wiggaton, Fluxton, Alfington and Salston – derive their names from the Saxons. This certainly suggests the existence of an extensive and well-organised community that had as its focal point the village that was to become Ottery St Mary.

It was in 963 that Ottery's recorded history began. In that year King Edgar (959–75) granted to Wolfhelm a tract of land with its woods, meadows, pasture and fields in his Royal manor of Otheri. It is possible that Wolfhelm was a resident steward who managed the manor for the King. The manor would remain in the hands of the Crown until 1061 when Edward the Confessor, who had been brought up in Rouen and was more French than English, gifted the manor to the cathedral church of St Mary at Rouen which was then being rebuilt and was appealing for funds. The manor at Ottery was a large and wealthy one and its rent and taxes were valued in Domesday (1086) at £23 per annum, a figure that must be multiplied by around 2,000 to equate it with present-day money.

Domesday begins to put some flesh on the bones and tells us that Ottery had three mills and owned a salt-pan in Sidmouth. Its population was probably around 500, whereas Exeter had 2,000 inhabitants.

At the mouth of the River Otter, some six miles south of Ottery, lay the port at Otterton (until it silted up during the sixteenth century). There were as many as 33 salt-pans at Otterton in 1086 out of a total of 77

An aerial view of Ottery St Mary taken c.1950. Note the lack of development in the area to the left in front of the River Otter.

Salston House, c.1910. In 2004 it is the Salston Manor Hotel.

Salston Farm, c.1910. The dwelling is a private residence in 2004.

for the whole county of Devonshire, and it is possible that some of the salt trade passed through Ottery on its way to the rest of Devon. The town's Broad Street (The Square) lay at the junction of five roads, a common occurrence in many Saxon towns where a wide street at its junction with other roads formed the market-place.

The date of the building of Ottery's first church is not known, although there may have been a wooden building in the village quite early during its Saxon period. In 2004 St Mary's most likely stands on the same spot. By the mid-twelfth century Ottery undoubtedly had a church and St Saviour's Bridge was certainly in existence by 1355. Constructed of stone it did have a chapel built on it by Bishop Grandisson, and a will of 1524 leaves ten shillings (50p) for six lights at Saint Saviour's chapel. At the

St Saviour's Bridge, Ottery St Mary, during its strengthening and widening in 1992. The original bridge was built in 1851 and it is a scheduled ancient monument.

1280 the Dean and Chapter at St Mary's at Rouen obtained further privileges for the town of 'gallows and the assize of bread and ale.' It is not clear what the privilege of gallows implied, unless it was the right to try capital offences in the Manor Court. But the assize of bread and ale conferred further rights to control trading in the town, including that of being able to fine bakers for short weight or inferior bread and brewers for short measure or inferior ale. An ale taster figures among the town's officials as late as the eighteenth century when he was fined in the Manor Court for not ensuring that the public houses sold their ale and beer in standard measures. These rights, the market charter and the fairs are akin to the rights granted in charters conferring borough status on towns, but although Ottery St Mary never became a

eastern approach to the town was another chapel dedicated to the Celtic St Budeaux.

Undoubtedly, Ottery was a market town in Saxon times and, in 1227, the church of St Mary at Rouen established it as a market town through a petition to Henry III (1216–72). This charter gave them the valuable right to control the market, levy tolls on goods coming into the town and to rent stalls to traders, also giving the traders protection under the umbrella of the market laws. A right to hold fairs was also granted to the town through this charter. In

borough it is nevertheless apparent that by the latter part of the thirteenth century the town had a well-organised corporate structure and was truly a typical small market town. The population was around 600 with the preponderance of them living in the town and the others in the scattered settlements and farmsteads. Open fields to the east surrounded the medieval town of Ottery St Mary and the boundaries of these can still be seen on nineteenth-century maps. To the west and north were lush meadows bordering the river and East Hill and West Hill provided

Although a drawing of the factory, this picture is especially interesting because it also shows St Saviour's Bridge before it was realigned in the nineteenth century.

St Saviour's Bridge, Ottery St Mary, in the 1930s before it was widened in the 1990s.

common land for pasture and pannage (the right or privilege of feeding pigs on common land).

Ottery appears in the records again in 1283 when the notorious Walter of Lechlade, precentor of Exeter Cathedral, acquired the lease of the manor. His greed and extortion caused widespread discontent and he was murdered in the Cathedral Close a few months later. The vicar of Ottery was implicated in the murder and was imprisoned. Fortunately he could plead Benefit of Clergy and was eventually released. Others, including the Mayor of Exeter, were less fortunate and were hanged.

The attractions of Ottery as a place to live led to a number of wealthy and influential families settling in the manor whose presence enhanced its prosperity and standing. By the middle of the fourteenth century there were six country seats in the area: Ash, Cadhay, Escot, Holcombe, Knightstone and Thorne. Of these Cadhay and Knightstone remain as ancient buildings. Escot, for long the seat of the lord of the manor, was rebuilt in 1808 after its destruction by fire, but Ash, Holcombe and Thorne have long since disappeared, although the names of Holcombe and Thorne live on as farms. The town's manor-house lies behind the church but the medieval building was demolished and rebuilt in 1860.

In 1332 the Crown levied a tax on all heads of families, except for those who were very poor. The tax assessment for Ottery St Mary lists 134 names and this, allowing for evasion and exemption due to poverty, would correspond to a total population of the manor of some 750 people. Small though the town looks to modern eyes, it provided essential goods and services to the community. Thus, the occupations of the inhabitants included a miller, a smith, two tanners, a cooper, a tailor, a potter and a soap maker. The last individual would not have provided soap for personal hygiene but industrial soap for scouring fleeces and skins – a reminder of the importance of sheep in the medieval economy.

The Ottery Feoffees were founded as a Trust to minister gifts and money donated for the benefit of the poor. The foundation existed as early as 1440 and by the mid-sixteenth century had acquired a number of almshouses that still survive, albeit in new buildings, and which continue to be administered by the Feoffees. One group of almshouses was founded by William Sherman of Knightstone and the other by Robert Hone, who has a tenuous claim to fame through his daughter who married John Bodley of Exeter and whose son, Sir Thomas Bodley, was the founder of the Bodleian Library. The Feoffees continue their charitable works and in recent years they have established the Day Centre in the town for the elderly and the infirm.

By the sixteenth century Ottery St Mary had become an important market town and surviving returns for 1524 show that in that year the town ranked as 39th among English towns in terms of tax paid, with the tax assessments for the subsidy containing 250 names. Allowing for those who were exempt this represents a total population of perhaps 1,200 people throughout the parish. Regrettably only six individuals had their occupations given, but these coincidentally formed a representative cross-section: there was a fisher, a weaver, a cordwainer, a carpenter, a brewer and a butcher. The significance of Ottery in the economy of Devon is shown by the fact that, Exeter apart, the 250 taxpayers were exceeded in numbers only by Tiverton, Plymouth and Crediton. The Exeter roll has 800 names, the city paying £365 in tax against Ottery's £79, almost a quarter as much. Of the 250 tax-paying families about half were wage labourers who had goods worth less than £2. At the other end of the social scale nine taxpayers were assessed on goods worth over £50.

At the dissolution the manor of Ottery was granted to Edward Seymour, Duke of Hertford, who was later executed for treason in 1552 when the manor reverted to the Crown. In 1610 it came into the ownership of Prince Henry, son of James I who died prematurely aged only 19 in 1612, and later it devolved on Prince Charles (Charles I, 1625–49).

The response of an Ottery jury in 1612 to a questionnaire about the manor's customs and assets survives and gives a glimpse of life at that time. There were three mills: the ancient town mill, Tipton Mill and the newly erected mill belonging to Mr Richard Sherman. The tenants had the right of pasture for their sheep and cattle on 'the two great wastes', one called East Common, the other West Common, and they also had freedom to fish and to fowl in the River Otter. Rather surprisingly there was only one small area of woodland and there were no quarries of stone or other minerals. There was a weekly market and three fairs a year. The bounds of the parish and manor were set out and correspond with those of the 1061 charter of Edward the Confessor (1042–66).

The Calendar of State Papers tells us that in 1618 one Owen Evans, a messenger of the Star Chamber, arrived in Ottery St Mary pretending to have a commission to press maidens for the Bermudas and Virginia as part of a campaign to provide wives for the predominately male colonists. He is said to have frightened away 40 girls 'who fled to such obscure places that their parents cannot find them.' However, in return for a bribe of ten shillings (50p) he agreed to exempt the parish. He was clearly operating a scam and was apprehended shortly afterwards.

We come now to the great upheaval of the Civil War. Ottery St Mary was a Royalist town and Royal troops under Sir Richard Grenville were billeted there in 1645, where he made himself thoroughly unpopular, raising money by force and, according to a contemporary account, 'indulging in arbitrary and dictatorial excesses'. As the fortunes of war changed Grenville was followed in October 1645 by Sir Thomas Fairfax (with Henry Ireton and John Pickering) and his Parliamentary army, en route to take Exeter. Fairfax lodged in Chanter's House, one of the old college buildings, where he had a meeting with Oliver Cromwell and held a convention in an attempt to recruit troops. A room encased in the Victorian rebuilding of the Chanter's House is said to have been the one in which they met. Cromwell received such little support from the local inhabitants

in his attempt to raise funds and troops for his army, and was so incensed by this, that he ordered his men to destroy the stained glass and ornaments in the church. In December of that year the bubonic plague visited Ottery St Mary and there was heavy mortality among both the troops and the inhabitants (it is said that as many as seven or eight people died per day during the plague). The Parliamentary forces withdrew from Ottery St Mary and moved to Tiverton from where, in the spring of 1646, they launched their successful attack on Exeter.

In the latter part of the seventeenth century a group of Protestant dissenters established themselves in Ottery St Mary and held their conventicles in the Chanter's House. Originally there was certain amount of violence directed at them but in 1688 they built one of the first Nonconformist churches in the country, which is now the town's United Reform church. In 1715 it is recorded that there were as many as 700 Nonconformists in the town, which must have represented about half of the town's inhabitants. Higher education was denied to Nonconformists and this led to the foundation in 1752 of the Western Academy in Ottery St Mary, to provide education for Nonconformist ministers. In 1764 the academy moved to Bridport and later to Bristol where it remained for many years as the Western College, which was the training ground for Congregational ministers. The building in which the Academy was founded is now the Marist Convent in Broad Street.

By the seventeenth century the town had taken on its present urban layout. Essentially the entire existing street names were in existence by the 1680s with some going back much further – the name of Tip Hill, the road to Sidmouth, appears in a record dated 1407. From the early-eighteenth century it is possible to see the town in more detail. Ottery St Mary had for several centuries been basically a society in which the majority of the inhabitants were subsistent farmers or farm labourers whose families earned additional income from spinning, weaving and lacemaking. Some were full-time weavers and a few, who organised and co-ordinated this activity, became well-to-do clothiers. Among other trades, tanning and leather working, particularly shoe making, were well established and of some significance. It is interesting that as early as 1321 Richard de Ottery was made a freeman of Exeter in the trade of cordwainer. Among the town's officers were 'searchers and sealers of leather and green skins'. Within the parish in the mid-eighteenth century there were four water-powered grist-mills and malt-mills, and adjoining the river by St Saviour's Bridge were two fulling-mills which also served as leather mills, a dye house, at least one tan yard and at least one saw-pit. Together they formed quite a little industrial estate. A leather mill, it should be explained, was where chamois leather was kneaded with oil and scoured using the same stamps that were used in the fulling of cloth (fulling was the process in which cloth was cleaned and shrunk by heat, pressure and moisture). At the other end of the town was the 'rack-park' where cloths were stretched on frames to dry after fulling and dyeing. Among the 11 well-to-do Ottery St Mary tradesmen, who insured themselves with the Sun Insurance Company when it opened its Exeter office in 1722, were two serge makers, a tanner and a soap maker. By the middle of that century there were 27 Ottery St Mary serge makers insured with the Sun, some for amounts in excess of £500, which represented a sizable business.

The records of Ottery St Mary's Court Leet offer a few glimpses of conditions in the town. The way-wardens were repeatedly mentioned as failing to remove dung and refuse from the streets and for allowing the roadway to fall into disrepair. The court was constantly ordering householders to repair their chimneys that presented a fire hazard among the mainly thatched houses and, in 1738, it upbraided several people for keeping ducks within the town 'that were suffered to puddle and disturb the water running in a brook through Jesu Street to the great inconvenience of His Majesty's subjects.' Finally, in 1736, the court had the temerity to complain that the lord of the manor had not repaired the ducking-stool.

In addition to spinning and weaving, lacemaking was another significant trade in Ottery St Mary. Lacemaking was introduced from Italy during the reign of Elizabeth I and was flourishing in Honiton by 1630. So-called Honiton Lace was soon being widely made on a cottage-industry basis in East Devon. Perhaps surprisingly, a return of 1699 shows that Ottery St Mary was second only to Honiton as a lacemaking centre. There were as many as 814 lace-makers listed in the town compared with 1,341 in Honiton. The 814 Ottery St Mary lacemakers must have represented about half the population and so must have included most of the women and children, although many, of course, worked on a part-time basis. In the nineteenth century lacemaking was increasingly commercialised and it became notorious for exploiting child labour, and through so-called 'lace schools' children as young as five years old were taught the craft. A veneer of respectability was achieved by also teaching them to read.

It is said that lace which was made all over East Devon was called Honiton Lace because it was brought to Honiton for shipping to London. There the merchants would ask if the lace from Honiton (or the Honiton Lace) had arrived.

There must have been much poverty in the town by the eighteenth century as a workhouse capable of housing 200 poor people (about one eighth of the population) was built by St Saviour's Bridge in 1738 and remained open for 100 years until the building of a Union Workhouse in Honiton in 1838. In 1766 the less-than-affluent majority of the population rose in anger over the price of bread and, in the ensuing bread riots, totally destroyed one of the town's flour-mills and its machinery and also demolished Tipton Mill, two miles downstream. This incident nearly led to the turn out of the Exeter Militia.

Strife in Europe, culminating in the Napoleonic Wars, and the competition from East Anglian serges and from cotton textiles, led to a serious decline in the woollen-cloth industry in Devon. In an attempt to counter this depression in the cloth trade the joint lords of the manor, Sir George Yonge and Sir John Duntze, built Ottery's secular monument between 1788–92 – the factory (finally closed in 2003). This necessitated re-routing the mill leat, making a new millpond to give a sufficient head of water to drive an 18-foot wheel and installing a circular 'tumbling weir' to return the surplus water to the River Otter. This was a larger version of the so-called 'plug weirs' that had been designed by James Brindley for controlling water-levels in the Worcestershire and Staffordshire Canal c.1770. At the same time a new flour-mill was built which operated until 1937. Unfortunately, the factory was a financial failure. Initially it spun worsted thread, some of which went to Exeter Market and some to the carpet weavers of Kidderminster. Sir George Yonge became financially embarrassed in 1794, possibly contributed to by the factory venture, and it was offered for sale. It appears that it attracted no buyers and it is said that it lay idle between 1796–1801. However, it then resumed woollen spilling until 1824 when it was converted into a silk-mill. In 1838 it employed 325 people and was the major source of employment in the town. It was sold in 1882 and by the end of the century was occupied by a firm of chemical manu-facturers and bottlers of beer and mineral water, and later such diverse activities as brush making and shirt-collar making, as well as the manufacturing of cardboard sleeves for gramophone records. Eventually, in the mid-1900s, it passed to Ottermill Switchgear and was later owned by Cutler Hammer, an American electrical company.

During the Napoleonic Wars temporary barracks were built in what became known as Barrack Road just outside the town on the Exeter Road. Troops from a wide area were billeted there including men from Somerset, Bedfordshire, Buckinghamshire and Hampshire. The parish registers show that a consid-erable number of them married local girls. The Volunteer public house in Broad Street dates from this period. Also, in the Napoleonic Wars, a signal station was built on West Hill on an unknown site, although it must have been near Daisymount Junction on the A30. It was one of a chain of semaphore stations linking Plymouth to London.

In the 1840s the population of Ottery was almost 4,500 and, from the Board of Health report of 1850, we get a comprehensive picture of the conditions in the town at that time. The preamble to the report says that:

In former years Ottery St Mary was the seat of a manu-facture of serges, woollens etc. But this has given way and been superseded by the manufacture of silks, which is now carried on a considerable scale. And in the same factory where the serges used to be made. These works are now in operation, and are more prosperous, and more extensive than at any period when they were devoted to [the] *manufacture of serges.*

Inventories of the machinery in the factory made in 1796 and 1815 show that it housed only spinning-machines and the statement that it made serges is mistaken.

The report also says that Ottery St Mary had the reputation of being one of the best dairy-farming districts in the country. Powhele's description written in the 1790s describes the orchards and gardens skirting the lower part of the town and the verdant fields and hedgerows elsewhere. He also complemented Ottery St Mary as being 'a place of some eminence'.

However, Ottery St Mary was not an idyllic country town and the health statistics are daunting. The average age at death was 24 years and almost one in three children died under the age of five. Half of the deaths were due to epidemic, endemic and contagious diseases. The farm labourers were a depressed class – many were unemployed during the winter and relied on hand-outs of grain from the farmers for food, which were debited against future wages. They lived, we are told, chiefly on potatoes, turnips and bread and could seldom, if ever, buy meat. The sanitary conditions of the town were appalling. Not only were there no drains but also, in many cases, the houses of the poor were without privies. Where sewage was carried off, it was achieved by means of open streams and gutters, many of which led into the town brook that ran along the line of Brook Street and Hind Street. In an area containing 228 houses there were 58 pigsties, stables and cowsheds that discharged into the brook and, eventually, into a 'mud pit' near where the fire station stands in 2004. This was emptied once a year and the contents spread on the fields. Drinking-water came from five pumps and a charge of a penny a quarter was levied on householders to keep them in repair. When the local residents defaulted on payment the handles were locked. Predictably, the cesspits of the more prosperous houses are said to have seeped into the wells.

The mill employed 325 people in 1839 and the overcrowding of the poorly paid workers was appalling, with up to 12 adults living in one room. In Sandhill Street one room 15 by 13 feet contained four beds and was occupied by a family of six people and, incredibly, by a lodger.

However, all was not gloom – in the same period the far-sighted lord of the manor, Sir John Kennaway, began to encourage the reclamation of common

ground on West Hill to provide smallholdings, which were let for a small rent subject to good husbandry being observed. From being a virtually uninhabited waste, West Hill soon supported a growing popula-tion. Kennaway gave the land for a church that was consecrated in 1846, with a school following in 1876. West Hill had extensive oak plantations that provided bark for the town's tannery as well as timber. They were completely felled during the First World War to provide props for trenches and dugouts. West Hill also had its own flour-mill, that was still operating within living memory, and also a leather mill. It is now a thriving and growing suburb of Ottery St Mary.

Unfortunately, few of the town's old buildings survive because of several disastrous fires. One, in 1587, destroyed the King's School and 13 houses, another, described as a 'painful pre-eminence of conflagration', occurred in 1604. The parishioners of Heavitree contributed the sum of 16 shillings (80p) by way of relief and those of Tiverton £3.14s. Other fires followed in 1765 and 1767 that centred around the market-place and consumed over 50 of what were described in the *Exeter Flying Post* as the most principal houses of the town. Many of the houses in this area date from a rebuilding that immediately followed these fires. The major fire of 1866 destroyed most of the town's main streets and consumed 111 houses before the combined efforts of Ottery St Mary's fire-engine and three fire-engines from Exeter eventually brought it under control. It was national news and was reported in the *Illustrated London News*. As a result of this confla-gration most of the buildings are post-1866. One notable building that survived was Raleigh House, built in 1806 on the site of an earlier house, which Polwhele says was once a home of Sir Walter Raleigh. There appears to be no evidence for this and it may be purely coincidence that among the wealthiest of the town's taxpayers in the 1524 Lay Subsidy Rolls was a Joan Ralegh who was assessed at the considerable sum of £90. This house was the home of Dr Edward Davey who was a pioneer of the electric telegraph and who invented an electrical relay and a needle telegraph before he emigrated to Australia. All his apparatus was destroyed in the 1880s and his contribution to telegraphy remains largely unrecognised.

By the middle of the nineteenth century Ottery St Mary had become a self-sufficient market town. The major employer was still the factory originally built by Sir George Yonge and Sir John Duntze, but there was a flourishing tannery supplying leather to the town's 17 boot and shoe manufacturers. At that time there were also nine tailors, ten bakers, six or seven butchers, five blacksmiths, four wheel-wrights, ten grocers, a book seller, six physicians and three chemists and druggists. A Town Hall was built in 1860 by popular subscription to provide 'an ornament' to the town. This stands in the Flexton (or Market Place) outside the church – in 2004 it houses the town's library.

Societies were appearing – there was a Library and Lecture Society, the Ottery St Mary Working Men's Mutual Improvement Society and a Mutual Aid Society. A Hand-Bell Ringers Society appeared in 1850, a cricket club in 1858 (which makes it one of the oldest in Devon) and a Choral Society in 1869. The Oddfellows had established an Ottery St Mary branch in 1844 and in 1895 the Institute was built using bricks from the Ottery Brickworks that lay at the foot of East Hill and functioned until 1969. Main drainage came in 1852 along with piped mains water, a gasworks was built in 1865 and the railway came in 1874. Before the railway arrived stagecoaches picked up passengers at the Fairmile Inn on the northern boundary of the parish and the town itself also possessed several posting inns. Water turbines that were installed in the factory in 1912 generated the town's first electricity for domestic lighting; street lighting followed soon afterwards.

The town's medieval bridge (St Saviour's) had been swept away by floods in 1801 and its replacement was similarly destroyed in 1849. The 1851 replacement, the present bridge, is made of cast iron and stands on a new alignment, and is scheduled as an historic monument. Its arches were cast in Yorkshire and shipped by sea from Hull to Exeter.

The spiritual well-being of the town was catered for by a spate of church buildings. Anglican churches were built at Escot, Tipton St John, West Hill and Alfington and the well-known Victorian architect William Butterfield 'beautified' the Parish Church of St Mary. A Methodist chapel had been built in 1829 and the Baptists had one by 1845. There had been private schools before 1800, but national schools were built later for girls (1867) and boys (1868). A cottage hospital followed in 1870, built entirely at the expense of Mrs Isabella Elliot, one of the town's benefactors, who maintained it at her own cost for 22 years. A fine new hospital was built in the early-twenty-first century on the outskirts of the town, and the old hospital is in the hands of developers who are converting it to residential use at the time of writing.

The town's heyday was probably the period between 1850–1900 but, as the twentieth century progressed, Ottery St Mary began to lose its identity and self-sufficiency, mainly because many of the traditional trades disappeared and in 1974 it ceased to be administered by its own Urban District Council and fell with the ambit of East Devon District Council. Tragically all the UDC records were consigned to a skip, together with much memorabilia, and a slice of Ottery St Mary's recent history disappeared.

The Conservation Area Appraisal for Ottery St Mary published in 1999 stated that:

More than most settlements in East Devon there is evidence of under use, vacancy and dilapidation of historic buildings... in some parts of the town there is a pressing need for capital expenditure on historic build-ings and environmental improvements. This should be able to be justified as a result of the town having considerable tourist trade and a programme of suitable repair and enhancement would undoubtedly encourage potential and help in discovering the best means of interpreting the town's important history.

The Ottery St Mary Heritage Society is a sign of the renewed interest in the town's history and, hopefully, in due course it will in a position to establish a museum and an educational facility to raise aware-ness of Ottery St Mary's 1,000-year heritage. This is certainly its objective.

Ottery St Mary in the 1890s
Based on notes by the late Fred Baker

In 1890 I was living with my parents at their little greengrocer's shop close to the entrance of Silver Street. Two steps led down into the shop, and when the Teap Stream, otherwise known as the Town Brook, flooded, being open and spanned by a small bridge in those days, my father had to board and clay up the front door. The property was later pulled down, and it became a redbrick building numbered 3 Silver Street, and was Messrs Huxtable & Streat's boot and shoe shop for many years.

In my early days I can remember as a little boy sitting on Policeman Pike's lap at the old Police Station. One of the places on his beat when he had to meet up with another constable was at the Iron Bridge on the A30 near Fenny Bridges, and on the way, inside the gate at Four Elms Farm, was a jar of cider. Half to drink on the way out, the other half to drink on the way home! On another night when on his patrol he walked up Chineway as far as the outskirts of Farway and back, leaving at 9p.m. and returning at 6a.m. There were three policemen stationed at Ottery St Mary, and they all carried canes, and we knew it when they chased us.

On Tuesday my parents sent me to Exeter by train, half fare of course, with about 60lbs of butter from the local farmers for sale in the market there. Mr Harry Lovering took me in his cab from the London Hotel to Ottery railway station, and on my arrival in Exeter a barrow-man took me from the station to the market. My mother went there on Fridays with more butter and picked up the money. Incidentally she was the first person to sell tomatoes in Ottery St Mary. They were known as 'love apples' at the time. In later years when I followed my parents' occupation I brought the first grapefruit into the town.

Before the Jubilee Monument was erected in 1897 at the top of Church Hill [now Silver Street] I can remem-ber when a Dr Sequay came to town and, after gathering a large crowd at the top of the hill, he proceeded to sell his

PHOTOGRAPH:
HENRY BADCOCK

PHOTOGRAPH:
ALBERT WAY

Henry Badcock and Albert Way were both Ottery St Mary photographers during the late-nineteenth century. Badcock's studio in Broad Street is the site of Life Style Pharmacy in 2004, while Mr Way's is now a private residence. The subjects are unknown but the two ladies' hats are nothing less than magnificent.

Left: *Two young and unknown Ottery girls pose, c.1890.*

Above: *Mrs Baker working in the garden in Hind Street that she rented from Lord Coleridge, 1917. Her husband Fred sold much of her produce in his greengrocers' shop in Silver Street. In 2004 the Hind Street car park occupies the site of the garden.*

Left: *Mrs Baker poses proudly beside a selection of her prize-winning standard produce.*

wares. He was a Yankee, and had a wagon on which he hung treacle buns. Boys, with their hands behind them, were invited to compete by eating these sticky, swinging buns. The men had competed to find the first to smoke a pipe-full of tobacco. The prizes awarded to the winners were a couple of buns for the boys and an ounce of tobacco, then about 4d, for the men.

After these antics he extolled his wares that comprised of Prairie Ointment and Prairie Oil. It was claimed that the lame could walk down steps, and so on, after such treatment. But the effect soon wore off.

Money was scarce in those days and a farthing (960 of them in a pound) for sweets was a wonderful treat. I fetched skimmed milk, which cost a penny a quart, from Mrs Luxton on Tip Hill. A haircut at barber Ford's also cost one penny. We did a bit of mumming to earn a copper or two and also made our own ripraps and squibs for 5 November. We could buy a quarter of a pound of gunpowder at Mr Hew's shop in Broad Street and then wait until midnight to let off our cannons and blunder-busses [try that today and you would up spending a night in the cells]. *My mother made tea for the boys and the policemen that night – there were no coffee shops in those times.*

The Christmas market was a special occasion, part of it being held in the Flexton. Sheep were penned along the College Road [now known as The College] *and cattle and sheep were sold in Broad Street. The hurdles for the pens were kept in an old building near the entrance to The College. It was also used as a temporary lock-up for drunks until the police could deal with them.*

At the same spot by the churchyard wall, the water cart was filled from the stream or runlet (Dabbs Brook) so as to water the streets and keep the dust down. Excited children often ran behind washing their hands in the spraying water and getting thoroughly wet. The repair of the roads was put out to tender, and I recall the occasion when a steamroller ran away on Corn Hill, and crashed into a house in Gold Street. The Ottery St Mary Urban District Council had been formed in December 1894 with nine members, and the only two people employed by the council were Mr Squire, who acted as the town clerk, treasurer and surveyor, and Mr Tolman as road sweeper.

Before the telephone was available in the town, I remember when a fire broke out in Mill Street one night, a man dressed in only his pyjamas rode to Exeter on his motor bike to obtain help. The Ottery St Mary fire engine consisted of a two-handled pump mounted on a small truck with four wheels that was kept in a sandstone cave in the West Cliff at the top of Tip Hill.

During the Boer War a soup kitchen was run in Broad Street behind Mr Cripp's butcher's shop, and people from all around the town brought their basins and other containers for the welcome hot drink. What wild rejoicings took place when Ladysmith, and then Mafeking, were both relieved in 1900. The tradesmen stood around in Broad Street firing their guns and banging away; when peace was finally negotiated in

1902, the people of Ottery St Mary collected money and presented a gold watch to each of the two men who belonged to our local Volunteers and had served in South Africa. The presentation took place outside the London Hotel in front of a crowd of Ottregians who cheered the two heroes.

Ottery St Mary had a good rugby team in those days, and on one occasion I went to see them play at Newton Poppleford, a trip that cost me two pence return to Tipton St John and then walked the rest of the way along the Exmouth line which was then in the process of being constructed. On a Bank Holiday I went to Sidmouth (four pence return) and the train was so full of passengers on the return journey that it had quite a job to get up the incline towards Harpford Wood at Bowd. We boys got out and ran along beside it and then jumped back on again as it chugged on downhill towards Tipton St John station.

What is now Barclay's Bank plc in Silver Street was formerly a chemist's shop with huge glass bottles filled with bright coloured liquids displayed in the window. This bank was originally in Cornhill when it was the London and South Western Bank and it was the first bank to be opened in the town.

In those days, Silver Street, Gold Street, Church Hill, the Flexton and Cornhill formed the busy centre of the town, with the Town Hall, built in 1859–60, providing a suitable place for Petty Sessions, and other public purposes, a retiring room, a library, a reading-room, and a more convenient market that replaced the old Market House that had become derelict.

From 1907 the old Ottregian Society arranged rail trips from Waterloo to Ottery St Mary on Whit Monday, the return fare being six shillings and six pence (just under 33p). There was an occasion when almost 1,000 people made the journey in two special trains that arrived at 6am and left for London at 6pm. And now no trains at all to Ottery St Mary – such a pity!

On Sunday afternoons people were permitted to walk through the grounds of Chanter's House, and on through Dunkirk beyond Hind Street. The big house (Chanter's) had several servants including a butler and a footman. At that time a carriage and pair could be hired from Honiton.

We moved to number 21 Silver Street at the top of the hill where my wife and I carried on the business of florists and greengrocers. For many years I rented a site in The College upon which the original King's School had stood, and we used this as a market garden in connection with our business.

Bernard, Lord Coleridge, the second Baron, often took an evening stroll along The College, and would stop and have a few friendly words with me. He used to read the lessons at Matins on Sundays at St Mary's, and I welcomed his rich golden voice that was much admired. He was High Court judge from 1907–23. In 1951 I purchased the garden in The College of which I had been the tenant and had a house built there for our retirement.

Time flows on in a ceaseless cavalcade, so, before I forget, I have attempted to save some of these faded memories of long ago. There have been many changes in the Ottery St Mary that I once knew, and a number of places are no longer there. There were four black-smith's shops in the town and corn was still being ground at the mill until 1937. We have lost our magis-trates court and the police station has moved from the Priory and is now situated in the Flexton. Cattle markets that once attracted the farmers from the surrounding districts on Mondays are no longer held here and the Railway Inn near St Saviour's, the Five Bells in Mill Street and the Half Moon in North Street have all gone.

Since Mr Baker wrote these notes, Ottery St Mary has also lost the Plume of Feathers in Yonder Street and the Masons Arms in Sandhill Street. Along with these pubs, many of the names above the old Ottery St Mary shops have also vanished into history. Fred Baker died on 4 October 1976 aged 92 years.

The Old Ottregians Society

In the above notes Fred Baker recalled that six young Ottregians living in London at the time formed The Old Ottregians Society in 1898. From 1907 the Society arranged rail trips from Waterloo to Ottery St Mary on Whit Monday to meet up with old friends and celebrate what had become known as Ottery Day. He says that there was an occasion

when 1,000 people made the journey in two special trains that arrived at 6a.m. and left for London at 6p.m. This same figure is quoted by most authori-ties. If this is correct, it is of great interest that a town like Ottery St Mary (where apart from the factory, agriculture was the main employer) had nearly 1,000 former inhabitants of the town (and there must have been several who did not make the journey) who were working in the capital. A good claim could be advanced that this was a contributory factor as to why the population of Ottery St Mary dropped from 4,110 in 1861 to 3,495 by 1901.

The Society flourished until the Second World War but decreasing membership, especially after the death of the secretary, Sidney Herbert Godfrey, hastened its closure in 1948. Since then trend has been for people to drift into Ottery St Mary rather than away from it.

The Story of West Hill
(1843–1905)
By John Pilsworth

The village of West Hill has a relatively short history when compared with many Devon villages, most of which date back to the Domesday Book (1086). The 1843 tithe map of the area shows West Hill as part of the Fluxton tithing and as a rural district of Ottery St Mary. At this time there was no church, school or inn – all usually associated with a village. Unfortunately,

Mr Potter, the West Hill blacksmith, c.1910. For such a tiny hamlet (at the time) West Hill appears to be over-staffed as far as postmen go; one is delivering a letter, presumably to Mr Potter, while a second is emptying the letter-box in the background.

Front and rear views of the Youth Hostel in Lower Broadoak Road, West Hill, c.1940. The hostel closed in 1955.

there were no named houses on this map. In 1843, Sir John Kennaway owned all the land at West Hill and the houses and cottages were invariably leasehold.

Change came to Victorian West Hill with the completion of St Michael's Church in 1846 and the opening of West Hill School in 1876. By most definitions of a typical village, West Hill seems only to date back to those times. In 1889 the Ordnance Survey map showed about 60 dwellings in the village – there were seven large houses at this time including West Hill Court, Bendarroch House, the first vicarage (approached from Toad Pit Lane), the Gap, Hawthorn Dene (called Mariners in 2004), Fir Grove and Summercourt. The named farms on the map were, Brickhouse, Castle, Highland, Perry's and Primrose. There were also seven or eight smaller farms and a few dozen farm cottages, many of cob construction. The smithy (where the supermarket stands at the time of writing), the mill (Foxenholes) and the Congregational chapel (now part of a house in Lower Broadoak Road) complete the list of buildings. The 1905 Ordnance Survey map of Ottery St Mary district shows West Hill village growing and new houses, such as Wurlie (now Elsdon House) and West Lodge.

The ten yearly censuses carried out from 1851 to 1901 provide information about household members, their occupations and places of birth. From 1851 to 1901 the number of households was steady at just over 70 and the population of West Hill varied between 332 and 358 during that 50-year period. In 1851, 80 per cent of the head of families worked on the land and the most frequently listed occupation was that of agricultural labourer, followed by farmer. By 1901 the number of heads of families working on the land had fallen below 40 per cent and there was a significant increase in the number of heads of families who were recorded as self-employed or professional. Between 1851–1901 the number of heads of families who were retired had risen from around four per cent to 15 per cent.

In 1851 and again in 1871 almost 95 per cent of the heads of families were born in Devon and over 60 per cent were born within five miles of Ottery St Mary. By 1901, 15 per cent of the heads of families were born outside Devon. The increase in the number of people born outside Devon could in part be attributed to the arrival of the railway in Ottery St Mary in 1874, giving people greater mobility.

A small school for infants existed at West Hill from about 1857. It was described as a Church Union School and was almost certainly provided by Sir John Kennaway on land adjoining a cottage known as Breaches, which he owned, between the village and Foxenhole Mills. The schoolroom was built beside the cottage (which is no longer there).

On 10 July 1876 the Ottery St Mary West Hill Board School opened with 49 scholars on the first day.

Foxenhole Mills, West Hill, in 1911. It stayed a working mill until the 1950s when it was developed as housing.

St Michael's Church, West Hill, c.1912.

The Post Office, West Hill, c.1906.

Cows killed by lightning at West Hill on 14 August 1914.

The West Hill branch of the British Legion (later Royal British Legion) in 1935. For such a tiny hamlet there were a lot of members.

Laying a wreath on John William Billiatt's grave in the 1930s.

The West Hill tug-of-war team, who were the winners of the Morrison Bell Cup at the British Legion Sports at Ottery St Mary on 21 May 1923.

West Hill, c.1908, looking towards Ottery St Mary with the old Post Office on the left.

The schoolmistress, Mrs Griffiths, wrote in the school log for this day:

I could not commence lessons until about eleven o'clock owing to mothers dropping in to assist with the children. They are all dreadfully backward with many of them not even knowing how to hold a pencil correctly.

The following year, Miss Mary George, aged 26 and from Victoria, Australia, took charge of the school and moved into the schoolhouse. Numbers were now in the sixties and by 1881 an assistant schoolteacher, Elizabeth Hurley, had been appointed. In December 1884, seven years after her arrival, Mary George returned to Australia. It is worthy of comment that West Hill had this Australian connection some 12 years before John Billiatt arrived. It would be nice to think that he came here on her recommendation, but there is no proof of that.

January 1885 saw the appointment of Mr John Sharland Cole as headmaster; he was trained at Exeter DT College and brought his wife Elizabeth with him to take the sewing classes. Miss Hurley was still the assistant teacher at the school where the numbers were now around 75. In 1890 the staff was increased to four following the appointment of Miss Florence Athwooll from North Devon as another assistant mistress. Mr Cole wrote in the school log soon afterwards, 'there have been several complaints about Miss Athwooll using a stick. I advised her to discontinue to using it and she promised to do so.' Her appointment had been necessary because numbers had nearly reached three figures but, in 1892, Miss Burrow replaced Miss Athwooll.

In July 1892 Mr Cole left to take up a post at Crookham School in Berkshire and Mr John Henry Jackman took charge. Mrs Jackman was responsible for knitting and needlework. In his first week at the school Mr Jackman lamented in the school log that 'the attendance of 91 was less because the harvest was not yet finished.' In 1901, at the end of the Victorian era, he was still in charge with his wife and two other assistant mistresses teaching over 100 children.

The school is still there in 2004 but it has moved to a new site behind Potter's Country Market. West Hill itself has grown out of all recognition and it has become a dormitory village for Ottery St Mary and even Exeter.

Escot

Mention Escot and most people think of Escot House, the home of the Kennaway family and Sir John Kennaway who was created a baronet by George III (1760–1820) in 1991. But there is more than that to the tiny hamlet to the north of Ottery St Mary – much more. Although it is a working rural community, and looks it, the houses and farms dotted around the tiny River Tale that rises in the foothills of the Blackdown Hills above Broadhembury, include much cob and

thatch and many splendid trees with, in season, a riot of wild flowers. The Church of St Philip and St James the Less stands away from the road in the middle of a field within the Escot House park and is quite close to the new dual carriageway A30 trunk road. Standing a few yards away is the only remaining tree of those that the protesters climbed into when the road was cut through a small copse. The most well-known of the protesters enjoyed brief national notoriety under the name of Swampy, but there are two things to ponder about over the incident. The first is that the much-needed road was built despite their protests and, secondly, that most of the protesters came from anywhere but Devon.

The building of St Philip and St James began in August 1868, the foundation-stone being laid by Sir John Kennaway, the second baronet. It was consecrated on 11 June 1844 and the Revd Douglas was installed as perpetual curate. In 1868, under the District Church Tithe Amendment Act, the incumbent became a vicar and remained so until 1958, when the Rector of Talaton became the Vicar of Escot

The Right Honourable Sir John Kennaway, Bart., CB, MP, photographed at the time of the 1906 general election. The picture was taken by W.D. Badcock who was a well-known Ottery chemist and photographer in Broad Street.

and Priest-in-Charge of Clyst Hydon and Clyst St Lawrence.

There is a school of thought among church visitors that a building has to be old to be beautiful. They should go to Escot where the Parish Church has a simple, plain beauty and two stained-glass windows on the south wall of the nave that would not look out of place in the grandest cathedrals in the land. They are attributed to the celebrated artist Henry Holiday who painted Dante and Beatrice in the Liverpool Walker Art Gallery. Outside in the churchyard snowdrops flourish in January and February, but it is doubtless pure coincidence that one of the windows has a snowdrop border. It cost £43 and was paid for by two friends of Miss Emily Charlotte Kennaway, Miss Vyvyan and a Miss Smith, in her memory.

The other window depicts the Last Supper and was commissioned by Sir John Kennaway, the third baronet, in 1879. Many Kennaway family memorials (mostly brass) adorn the walls, including the stone one to the first baronet.

For 32 years the churchyard was a labour of love to Jim Pearcy, who kept it neat and tidy almost to the point of being pristine. A total of 22 of his relatives are buried there and it is a lucky person, indeed an honoured one, who is taken on a personally conducted tour of the church by Jim.

The original Escot House was built for Sir Walter Yonge of Colyton between 1680 and 1688. According to legend, in the middle of the work some of the workers downed tools. It was not a union dispute, rather that they had a few days off to support the Duke of Monmouth's ill-fated rebellion. Those that survived Sedgemoor were captured and taken to Exeter for trial. They were sentenced to death

The Escot estate sawmills in 1908.

and brought back to Talaton and hanged, drawn and quartered at a crossroad where their dismembered bodies were left to rot on a gibbet. Ever since, the crossroad, to the east of Talaton on the Feniton road, has been known as Bittery Cross – or so the story goes.

Sir Walter had entertained the Duke of Monmouth when he visited Devon a few years earlier and it was said that men were hanged almost on his doorstep as a reminder of the fact, and also as a warning to him to keep his nose clean in future. On occasion a ghostly man with a horse and cart has been seen near Bittery Cross, supposedly carrying the rebels to their death.

George III, Queen Charlotte and three of their daughters were entertained at Escot in 1789, no doubt when he was staying at Weymouth, his favourite watering-place from where, six years earlier, he had sallied forth to Axminster to visit Thomas Whitty's carpet factory.

George Yonge sold the Escot estate to Sir John Kennaway, Secretary of State for War, in 1794 but, around ten years later, the fine building was completely destroyed by a fire, which was thought to have started when the curtains in a dressing-room

The 25th Company, 3rd Devonshire Volunteers, at Escot House in 1874 under Sir John Kennaway MP, the commanding officer. Corporal Fisher, a member of the company in 1870, presented the picture to the Drill Hall at Ottery St Mary.

Above: *Escot House in 1905, which is the home of John Michael Kennaway in 2004.*

Left: *Escot House Lodge in 1914.*

The Church of St Philip and St James the Less at Escot in 1910.

Above: *Escot villagers going to the celebrations for the coronation of George VI in 1937.*

Right: *Escot choir, 1951. Left to right, back row: Jack Selway, Frank Bastin, Revd Chapple, Alan Tratt, Jeff Wynn, Donald Wynn; front row: Jim Pearcy, Dennis Bastin, Henry Gosling, John Cooper, Mike Coombes, John Oxenham.*

The Church of St Philip and St James the Less at Escot in the 1990s.

were set alight by a candle. Thirty years later the house was rebuilt by Sir John's son, the Sir John that built the Church of St Philip and St James the Less.

The Kennaway family still live at Escot at the time of writing, and it has been turned into an aquatic park complete with wetlands and wildfowl – not to forget a troupe of wild boar.

The creation of the new A30 means that Fairmile and its Fairmile Inn have been bypassed and live out the years in quiet seclusion. It was not always so, being on the busy London to Exeter via Dorchester and Honiton coach run and the spot where passengers for Ottery St Mary left the main coach and either walked to the town or caught a lift with one of the carriers.

Why is it called Fairmile? We can ignore the fables which say that it is so called because 'it was a fair mile from Ottery St Mary', or because a Royalist fleeing from Oliver Cromwell reached that spot and collapsed, shouting 'I give in, but you had to chase me a fair mile before catching me.' The latter probably stems from the apocalyptic story that Cromwell killed two Royalist soldiers. The truth is more mundane because, in the cold light of dawn, and long before Cromwell, we find a reference to 'faire mile' in 1425, which suggests that there was an especially good part of the main Exeter road, which otherwise was little more than a track.

At this point it might be of more than passing interest to reflect that after the dissolution of the monasteries Henry VIII granted the manor of Ottery St Mary to Edward Seymour, Duke of Hertford, later Duke of Somerset, who was executed on flimsy charges of treason in 1552, when the manor reverted to the Crown. In 1610 it came into the ownership of Prince Henry, son of James I, who died prematurely aged only 19 in 1612, and later it devolved on Prince Charles (Charles I 1625–49). If Prince Henry had survived and reigned as Henry IX the Civil War

The Prince of Wales (later Edward VIII) passing through Fairmile on to his way to visit Ottery St Mary in the 1930s.

The Olympic Torch on its way to the London Olympic Games (1946) is being handed over at Fairmile.

Hare coursers meet outside Fairmile Inn, c.1920.

might never have taken place and Oliver Cromwell would have only a single line in the country's history and, most certainly, would never have visited Ottery St Mary.

Barely a mile to the east of Fairmile is Fenny Bridges, where the last agonies of the Prayer Book Rebellion took place in 1549. A ragged army of Devon and Cornish men lined up in a field known as Fenny Mead where they were beaten by a much better-equipped army under Lord Russell. But Devon and Cornish men never know when they are beaten and they regrouped and came back for another go at the King's men. They lost 1,000 men in all. The wounded were tended to in the manorhouse that was burnt to the ground as a reprisal. A further reprisal was carried out against the landlord of the inn (now called the Greyhound after the London coach that changed horses there). He had harboured some of the defeated army after the battle and was hanged, drawn and quartered outside his own inn. The Greyhound was virtually destroyed by fire in 1968 but a replica was built four years later.

One of the sparks that ignited the Prayer Book Rebellion landed at Clyst St Mary away to the east of Ottery St Mary when Sir Walter Raleigh's father, another Walter, heard an old woman complaining about having the new prayer book forced on her and other people. Walter Raleigh senr told her to grin and bear it and she rushed off to the Parish Church to tell the congregation what Raleigh had said.

The Fairmile Inn near Ottery St Mary, c.1908.

The Fairmile Inn at the turn of the century. On the left is the Post Office with its clock placed there to commemorate the golden jubilee of Queen Victoria (1887).

The Post Office at Fairmile in 1910.

The Greyhound Hotel at Fenny Bridges, c.1930. It gets its name from the Greyhound stagecoach that stopped there in former years.

A few moments later a lynch mob was rushing after him and he barely escaped with his life.

Along the old A30, halfway between the Greyhound and the Fairmile Inn, Patteson Cross, properly Spence Cross, takes it name from the wayside-cross monument to Bishop John Coleridge Patteson that stands on a small grassy island on the Ottery St Mary side of the road. His cousin, Lord Coleridge, placed it there in his memory, and its inscription reads:

In memory of John Coleridge Patteson D.D. Missionary Bishop. Born in London, 1 April, 1827. Killed at Nukapu near the Island of Samoa, 20 September 1871, together with two fellow-workers for our Lord, the Reverend Joseph Aitkin and Stephen Tarouiarao (in revenge for wrongs suffered at the hands of Europeans) by savage men whom he loved, and for whose sake he gave up his home and country and friends dearer than life. Lord Jesus grant that we may live to Thee like him, and stand in our lot with him before the throne to the end of the days. Amen. A kinsman desires thus to keep alive for aftertime the memory of a wise, a holy, and a humble man.

John Coleridge Patteson was the son of Mr Justice Patteson of Feniton Court who was ordained Deacon in Exeter Cathedral on 25 September 1853. Later he became the vicar of St James and St Anne's

The Patteson Memorial at Patteson Cross, near Ottery St Mary. In 2004 the memorial stands on a separate island.

Alfington Parish Church between 1853–55, from where he went to New Zealand to work under Bishop Selwyn among the islands of the South Pacific. In time he became Bishop of Melanesia between 1861 and his death in 1871. There is marble slab memorial to him at the west end of St James and St Anne's.

St James and St Anne's lies at the end of narrow lane just outside Alfington and on the left as you head for Honiton. It was locked the last time we visited it (February 2004) but, from earlier visits, it is recalled that there is a chancel and nave with a brick-built west tower. It is almost certainly kept locked because of the seventeenth-century French chalice and some seventeenth or eighteenth-century plate that is (was?) there. There is quite a bit of stained glass in the 11 lancet windows and the font in Devon marble is well worth a second look. Built as a chapel of ease in 1849 by the Hon. Justice Coleridge of Feniton Court, St James and St Anne's served as such until 1882 when Alfington was formed as a separate ecclesiastical parish and its church was consecrated in that same year.

The Coleridge influence is all around. As well as the Coleridge Patteson memorial, Lady Coleridge wainscoted the vestry, and a marble, alabaster and Caen stone monument was erected in 1902 to Lord Coleridge, Lord Chief Justice of England, who died in 1894.

Alfington village, Ottery St Mary, c.1908.

The Alfington Inn (the white building), *Alfington, on a post-card dated 11 March 1913.*

Alfington, c.1910.

Chapter 2

❖

St Mary's Church

Without doubt Ottery St Mary's crowning glory is its magnificent Parish Church of St Mary. Many claim it as the best Parish Church in Devon, although the people of Tiverton, Crediton and Colyton might have different views on that. Any argument in that direction has to include the much simpler but still superb St Winifred's at Branscombe. And not just for its idyllic setting.

It was Bishop Walter de Bronescombe of Exeter, whose influence on the churches in Devon was considerable, who consecrated a church in Ottery St Mary in 1259. The manor of Ottery was given to the Chapter of the Cathedral Church at Rouen by Edward the Confessor (1042–66) whose love of all things Norman would lead to '1066 and all that'.

The earliest suggestion of a church in the town came in 1154 when a certain William is shown 'as vicar of Ottrei'. The Revd Sidney Davis, probably the leading expert when it comes to St Mary's, states that we have to wait until 1260 for 'the first mention of any church in the parish (which was co-extensive with the manor).' This was in the Register of Bishop Bronescombe.

In 1327 John de Grandisson was consecrated Bishop of Exeter. He wanted to found an establishment that would become a seat of learning and, after looking around the immediate vicinity, his choice fell

The Coke Monument, St Mary's Church, in 1905.

upon Ottery St Mary at which, after long and protracted negotiations, he purchased the manor. They were costly negotiations as well, the Canons of Rouen extracting what Grandisson thought to be an exorbitant price. He told them in 1334:

You seem to demand a heavy, excessive, intolerable and, with all due respect, a ridiculous sum, which it unlikely anybody would pay or offer for all you possess in our diocese, which hardly pays you 140 marks [around £94].

Whether Grandisson paid the 'ridiculous sum' is uncertain, but he did purchase the manor on 13 June 1335 and, obtaining permission from Edward III (1327–77), he established his collegiate church at St Mary's, conveying the manor of Ottery 'with all its appurtenances [accessories] to the Warden, Canons, and other ministers of his new College.' Under the deed of foundation there would be a collegiate body of 40 members – the warden, the minister, the precentor and the sacristan were the most important. A precentor was the person who led the congregation in singing, a forerunner to the choirmaster we suppose, while the sacristan was in charge of the sacristy or the place or room in the church where the priest prepares for a service and where vestments are kept. Other members included four simple canons, eight choral vicars, eight secondaries (clerks), a master of grammar and eight choirboys.

Such a college was deserving of a bigger (and better?) church – Grandisson certainly gave it one which was grandly modelled on his own cathedral at Exeter. His legacy to Ottery St Mary stands, as it has done now for nearly seven centuries, gazing serenely peacefully down on the town and community it continues to serve.

That serenity was severely tried after the dissolution of the monasteries in 1545 when the wardens and canons handed over the keys to the King's commissioners in May. Afterwards the chapter house was pulled down, much of the stone finding its

St Mary's Church, Ottery St Mary.

The 1887 bell at St Mary's Church that was cast for Queen Victoria's golden jubilee.

The newer stocks at Ottery St Mary in the 1920s. What 'crime' Mr Way, the Ottery photographer, had committed is not known.

Above: Henry Godfrey (second from right) ran a shoe shop in Silver Street. He was also a member of the Godfrey family's team of bell-ringers.

The consecration of the Church Army's van outside St Mary's Church, c.1907.

The choir outside St Mary's Church, c.1936.

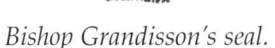

Bishop Grandisson's seal.

The Choir of the Collegiate Church of St Mary, at Ottery St Mary, in 1871. Left to right, back row: W.J.S. Rigby, G.S. Whitcombe, E. Carnell, F.D. Carnell, G. Streat, C. Gover, T.S. Digby, G.T. Channon; middle row: A.T. Warne; front row: G. Rendall, H. Streat, W. Wright, C.H. Whitcombe, J.S. Gover, L.Sharland, J. Pullman, J.W. Warne, F. Stuckey, E.R. Lippett, T.J. Carnell (organist).

The consecration of the ground used for the extension of the churchyard at St Mary's Church at Ottery St Mary on 23 February 1901. Lord Coleridge commissioned the conveyance on 23 May 1899.

Hand-bell ringers at Ottery St Mary in 1890. The three young ladies are thought to be the daughters of the vicar, Revd William Pryke.

The Ottery St Mary Church Choir in 1897, no doubt practising in readiness for the service that would mark Queen Victoria's diamond jubilee. Left to right, back row: J. Elliott, E. Carnell, F. Stuckey, F. Elliott, S.H. Godfrey, A. White, T. Channon, T. Whicker, H. Streat, A. Churchill, G. Turner, J. Baker; middle row: G.S. Dyer, W.J. Hooper, F.H. Stuckey, F.J. Streat, H. Drawer, J.N. Luxton, G. Toby, F. Salter, J. Streat; front row: R.L. Elliott, H.J. Hooper, A. Meldon, W. Lane (organist), T. Meldon, W. Dyer, W.D. Badcock, F.H. Streat, G. Berry (blower).

The foundation-stone laying ceremony by Miss Goodlad of the Church Institute at Ottery St Mary on 5 September 1895.

way to Cadhay and being used in building John Haydon's House there.

A later iconoclast, Oliver Cromwell, was refused financial aid and cash by the town and, according to legend, took it out on Ottery St Mary by destroying the statues and stained glass in the church and disfiguring the altar screen and the nave. His men even used the weathercock for target practice.

Thankfully a mid-nineteenth-century restoration put much of the earlier magnificence back and there is so much to see inside that the first-time visitor should allow two or three hours to take everything in. The first thing that strikes him is the size, even vastness, and an image that has added strength to it by the darkness.

The size is especially impressive when one looks down the magnificent (there is no other adjective possible) nave into the chancel. The nave is five-bayed with Bishop Grandisson's arms alternating with those of Montacute through the vaulting; the college benefactress, Catherine, Countess of Salisbury, had married William Montacute, Earl of Salisbury. The five bosses down the centre of the chancel include one that depicts the Blessed Virgin and Child. It is the last but one to the west and was featured on the 8d. stamp in the 1974 Christmas set, of which first-day covers sold freely in the town.

It is wise to avoid the church at night if you believe in ghosts. There is a much-admired effigy of Sir John Cole, who died aged 42 in 1632, between the Dorset aisle and the north transept. Standing life-size and in armour, he is said to suffer an uneasy conscience after murdering a brother for an inheritance and to ease that he comes down from his niche and prowls around inside the church.

The real treasure of the place is the west window, which is known as 'The Apostles' Window'. It depicts the 12 Apostles with their emblems – St Peter, for instance, is carrying the keys (of the Kingdom).

The rest? Go there and see it all for yourself, and make sure you buy a copy of John Whitham's excellent *The Church of St Mary of Ottery* on the way in.

St Mary's Church, Ottery St Mary, c.1890. Over the years the shrubs have been replaced, with headstones.

Vicars of St Mary's Church

1191	Peter the clerk
1191	Roger the chaplain
1283	John de Wolrington
1310	John de Thormerton
1329	John de Sharnebrok
1335	Oliver de Farsy

The collegiate church was founded on 22 January 1337 and ended on the dissolution of the college on 24 December 1545.

1550	John Bagster
1580	Ralph Mainwarynge
1590	Nicholas Forward
1626	John Forward
1660	Melchizdeck Alford
1691	William Hull
1692	John Rost
1695	– Burrows
1695	Thomas Gatchell
1713	Hugh Lewes
1713	Richard Jenkinson
1722	Ralph Farthing
1743	Richard Holme
1760	John Coleridge BA
1781	Fulwood Smerdon
1794	George Smith MA
1841	Sidney Cornish DD
1874	William Metcalfe
1890	Maitland Kelly MA
1900	William Emanuel Pryke
1908	John William Metcalfe
1920	Leonard Bristow Stallard
1938	Bernard Cecil Jackson
1950	David Rufus Price
1978	Peter John McGee
1996	Simon George Franklin

The hand-bell ringing team at St Mary's Church, Ottery St Mary, 1890.

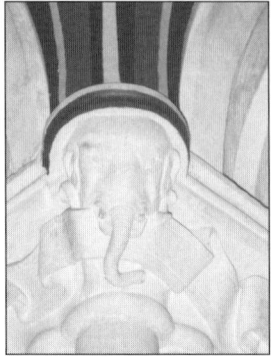

Above: *Ottery St Mary hand-bell ringers in 1889.*

Below: *The Grandisson Clock in the west wall of the transept at St Mary's Church, c.1930. Although it gets its name from John de Grandisson, the bishop between 1327–69 who built the church, John Whitham's* The Church of St Mary of Ottery *(1959) claims that during the course of six centuries the clock would have been considerably restored and that 'it is too much to claim that the essential structure is that of the Mediaeval horologe.'*

Above: *The elephant and the owl bosses in the nave at St Mary's Church.*

Below: *The workings of the medieval (1370) clock in St Mary's Church.*

John Haydon's tomb in St Mary's Church, c.1910. Sir John Haydon was one of the first four Governors of the Church in 1545. He died in 1587 and, in accordance with his request in his will, was buried in the north side of the choir. In that will he 'left forty shillings for the maintenance of the church and his sepulchre there.'

The nave in St Mary's Church, probably in Edwardian times but certainly pre-1934/35, when the niches at the side were placed there. The original altar was much defaced during the time of the dissolution of the college.

Bishop John de Grandisson.

St Michael the Archangel at West Hill

Priests in Charge

1846	James Thomas Boles
1848	Robert Henry Fortescue
1848	William Buckland Lott
1851	John Coventry
1857	Alexander Peter Turquand

Vicars

1868	Alexander Peter Turquand
1877	George Lloyd
1887	Thomas Hill Lowe
1924	Frank Perry
1943	Leslie Ernest Burgess
1952	Lewis H. Dukeswell
1959	Ernest C. Mortimer
1965	Douglas E. Hood
1974	Robert C. Lowrie
1982	Frederick G. Denman
1987	Ronald Burrow
1992	Patrick Nickols-Rawle
1998	Wenda Rioch

The Congregational Chapel

The Congregational Chapel (now United Reform Church) on the corner of Jesu Street and Batts Lane, c.1914.

Chapter 3

The Chanter's House and Cadhay

Samuel Taylor Coleridge's second-eldest brother fought in the Peninsular War, being appointed lieutenant colonel in the Exmouth and Sidmouth Volunteers in 1799. He married a local heiress, Frances Taylor, and bought Heath's Court, one of the better houses in the town and named as such after a previous owner until c.1900, although it was called the Chanter's House on its conveyance to the colonel. It goes without saying that it took its Chanter's House name from the fact that the chanter lived there during the time of the Collegiate College. Nothing survives today of the first medieval house, although considerable evidence was found when the service ranges were demolished in the nineteenth century. The last chanter to live there was John Peryans after the dissolution of the monasteries.

Oliver Cromwell met Sir Thomas Fairfax at the house in 1645 when Robert Collins, a staunch Parliamentarian, owned the house. A plaque on the dining-room door records this fact and that Cromwell demanded men and money from the people of the town.

Cadhay lies to the north-west of Ottery St Mary. It is a Tudor mansion built around a courtyard with entrances through each wing. There are statues of Henry VII and his three children, Edward VI, Mary I and Elizabeth I, in a niche above the entrances. Of special interest is the long gallery used for exercise during bad weather. The original Cadhay was built by the de Cadhay family in the thirteenth century; it passed by marriage to John Haydon who rebuilt it. By the beginning of the twentieth century the house had fallen into a state of some disrepair, but it was bought and restored by Dampier Whetham. It has since returned to the descendants of John Haydon.

The Chanter's House, Ottery St Mary, c.1920, when it was opened to the public for the first time. The chanter was responsible for leading the singing during divine services at the collegiate church. The house was renamed Heath's Court after being bought by Thomas Heath in 1685. In 1796 it was bought by James (later Lord) Coleridge and it is still in the family's hands. It went back to using its original name in the late-nineteenth century.

The tradition of the night-watchman, accompanied by three assistants, ringing the bell at Ottery St Mary on Christmas Eve dates back to the eighteenth century, although the first recorded night-watchman was George Godfrey in 1800. The ringing starts at the Chanter's House and takes in all the pubs and main buildings. Starting at midnight, the journey takes until 4a.m. to complete. The night-watchman for the 1991 ring was Nelson Owen, who is still in office in 2004 after first taking over in 1937. **Left to right:** *Chris Swindle, Ray Baker, Nelson Owen, John Godfrey, a descendant of the 1800 night-watchman.* PICTURE PUBLISHED BY KIND PERMISSION OF THE WESTERN GAZETTE, YEOVIL.

The library at the Chanter's House in 1926.

The Convention Room of Oliver Cromwell at the Chanter's House in the 1920s.

Below: *Cadhay House, Ottery St Mary.*

The Culmstock Otter-hounds meet at Cadhay Bridge on 21 May 1913.

Above: *Ottery St Mary Silver Band at Cadhay, c.1918.*

The workforce at Cadhay Farm, c.1932. Mr Burrow, the tenant of the farm, is on the extreme right.

Cadhay Crossing level-crossing gates looking towards Sidmouth Junction (now Feniton Station), c.1965, shortly before the Sidmouth branch line was closed. This has to be one of the very few photographs ever taken of these gates.

Above and right: *Over the years Head Weir had been allowed to fall into disrepair, restoration work being finally carried out in the 1950s.*

Chapter 4

The Pixies' Revenge

The Pixies' Revenge was based on their alleged failure in 1454 to destroy a bell that was made and installed in St Mary's Church. The bell was to be known as St Mary. The pixies were alarmed, after all a church bell to them has the same affect that Holy Water has to the Devil. They contacted their allies, the 'Nuggies' and 'Peddiwees' and others who live and work underground, and asked them not to supply any metal to the monks and their workers. They obliged, but it was only a delaying tactic, and eventually sufficient metal was gathered together.

Plan two was put into operation. This saw the pixies travel to the foundry at Exeter, gathering dew from flowers on the way. They crept in one by one so as not to arouse suspicion and dropped the dew into the cooling casting. This should have caused the casting to crack, but the flowers decided to put a stop to this and asked the bees to mix some honey with their dew. The result was that the casting was so improved that the bell had the sweetest tone heard in the area for many a long year.

Plan three was, as Baldric would have us believe in the TV series 'Blackadder', cunning beyond belief. They joined the monks carrying the bell to Ottery and beguiled them with stories and delicious water. In a trance the monks were led to edge of the cliffs at Sidmouth where, just before the whole lot went over the edge, Brother John trod on a thistle and woke from his trance, saving the day.

The final attempt was made just before the bell was to receive its blessing by the sexton. He checked the tower on the morning of the great day and found that the bell, and its striking parts, had been bound together by magic cords. A hasty breaking-of-the-spell ceremony was carried out and, at nine o'clock in the evening on Midsummer Day 1454 the bell rang out over the town.

Time has no meaning to pixies and they decided to wait for 500 years (1954) before taking their revenge on Midsummer Day (celebrated in Ottery as Pixies' Day). A true story? It depends on whether you believe in pixies or not, doesn't it?

Pixies' Day on Midsummer's Day, 1954.

Pixies' Day at Ottery St Mary in 1957. Posing in Hind Street are, left to right: David Ash, Gordon Down, Bert Horrel, Peter Harris, Derrick Croydon; front: Harold Phillips.

Pixies' Day, Midsummer's Day, 1954. Saying sorry was not enough for Mr Fred Godfrey; and who can blame the pixies, he was the man who thought up the whole idea. On the left of the picture is Sid Wills carrying his son Peter.

If the pixies did not like bells ringing in 1454 we wonder what they made of this lot 'Beating the Retreat' in Broad Street on Pixies' Day, 1954, 500 years later.

Below: *One or two of the younger spectators look on rather anxiously while the pixies capture the bell-ringers and take them to their 'cave' in Broad Street.*

Above: *The Pixies' Parlour on the banks of the River Otter where Samuel Taylor Coleridge (allegedly) wrote some of his poems.*

BUCKINGHAM PALACE

21st June, 1954.

Dear Mr. Adams,

Thank you for your letter, which I have had the honour of laying before The Queen.

Her Majesty thought it most kind of you to offer on behalf of your Committee two copies of your Pixie legend and two Ottre Pixie emblems for The Duke of Cornwall and Princess Anne. The Queen has much pleasure in accepting these for her children as a token of your good wishes.

Yours sincerely,

Lady-in-Waiting.

S.A. Adams Esq.,
    Pixies Parlour,
        Ottery St. Mary,
            Devon.

Above: *A royal thank you.*

A modern Ottery Day celebration.

Occasions

Above: *Broad Street celebrations for the coronation of George VI in 1937.*

Left: *Celebrations for the silver jubilee of George V in 1935 in Broad Street, the inevitable setting for most of Ottery's big days.*

Yonder Street's Coronation Party in 1953. Left to right: Mrs Boyland (behind), Rosena Bond, Revd Rufus Price, Lynda Blackmore, Mrs Bond. We wonder how many cakes the vicar had to eat that day as he visited every street party in turn.

The distribution of the mugs to mark the coronation of Queen Elizabeth II on 3 June 1953.

The celebrations in Broad Street at Ottery St Mary for the coronation of King George V in 1911.

E. W. BOYLAND,

WINDOW CLEANER,

Carpet Beating etc. undertaken.

Temporary Address:—

Brook House, Brook, Ottery St. Mary.

Orders promptly attended to

Charges moderate

Right and below:
The celebrations at Ottery St Mary for the coronation of George VI on 12 May 1937.

A decorated Sandhill Street prepares to celebrate the coronation of George VI in 1937.

The Women's Institute entry in an Ottery St Mary Carnival in the early 1950s. The driver with the enviable job of escorting this bevy of beauties is Ted Dyer.

Another WI Carnival entry, 1950s.

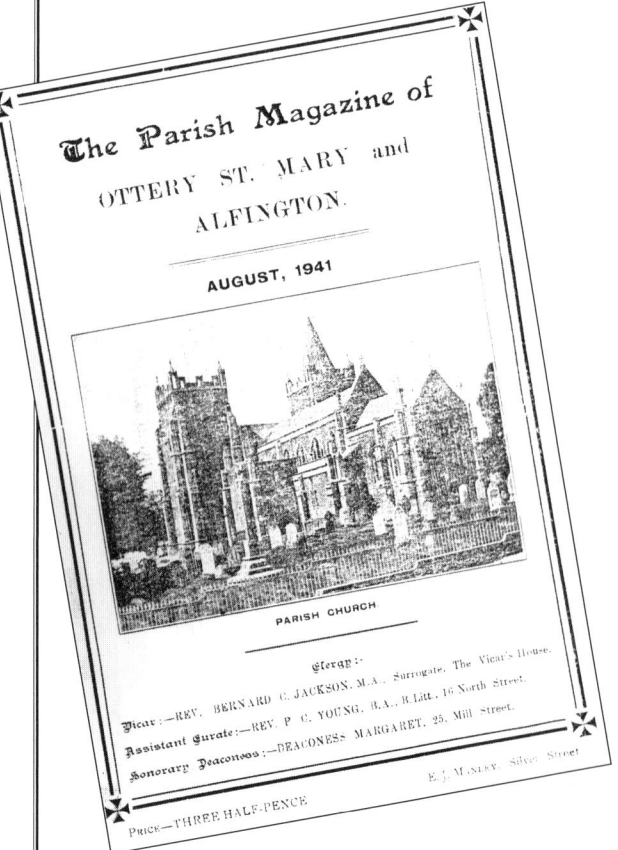

The Jolly Jesters' entry in the 1911 Ottery Carnival.

The Ottery St Mary Committee for the coronation celebrations of Edward VII (1901–10) on 9 August 1902.

The Ottery St Mary Committee for the coronation celebrations of George V (1910–36) on 22 June 1911.

Above and right: *Ottregians enjoying a street party to celebrate the coronation of George V in 1911. In 2004 the white building behind them is divided into the Crusty Cob bakery and the Devon Air Ambulance charity shop. The building in the background was Mr Williamson's draper's shop on the junction of Jesu Street and Tip Hill. It was destroyed along with most of Tip Hill in the great fire 1866 and not rebuilt until 1907. Since at least the 1930s it has been a fish-and-chip shop.*

The celebrations in Broad Street at Ottery St Mary to mark the silver jubilee of George V in 1935.

The line up for the start of Ottery St Mary's 1958 Carnival Pram Race. Left to right, pushers: Paul Vicary, Eddie Whitcombe, Nelson Owen, Derrick Croydon, Bert Horrel, David Ash; babies: Gerald Woodley, Peter Bull, Tony Bastyn, Harold Lovering, Peter Harris, John Paddon.

Gerry Totterdell with the blazing tar barrel and Peter Ayres behind him during the 'Rolling of the Tar Barrels' at Ottery Carnival in the 1950s.

Tar Barrel Rolling at Ottery Carnival in 2001. The Midnight Barrel (below) that finishes the evening's entertainment is bigger than the normal barrels and requires two men to handle it.

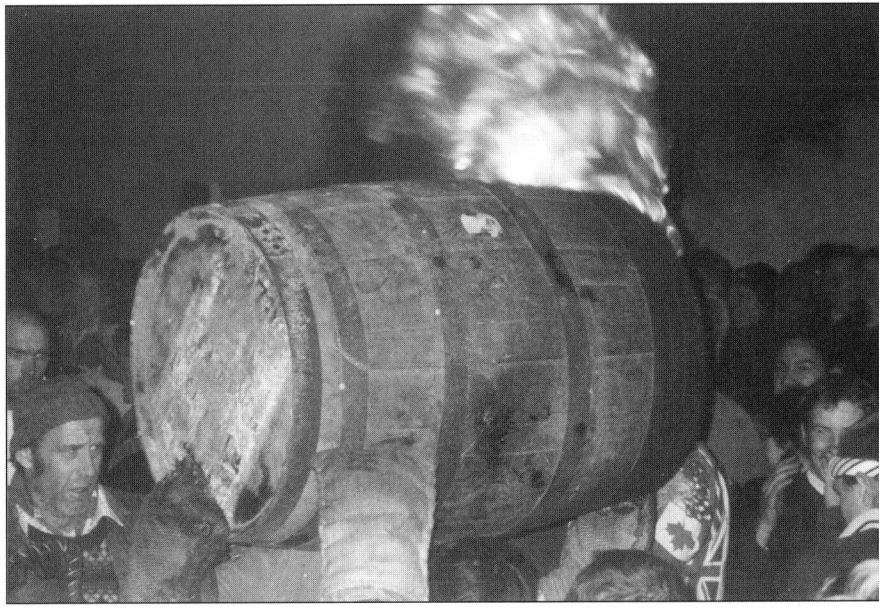

Jenny Carter was the Ottery St Mary Carnival Queen in 1952.

Mrs Denning crowning Marjorie Paddon as Carnival Queen in the 1950s. Left to right, back row: Mary Hellier, Mrs Denning, ?, Olive Rowland; front row: Enid Hutchings (attendant), Marjorie Paddon, Pearl Salter.

The 'Traffic Jam', an entry in the Ottery St Mary Carnival in 1931. Eric Parsons is in the pedal car, Dennis Dunsford is fourth from the right and Mr Lathrop, the gasworks manager is on the far right. The lorry belongs to the Foxenhole Mills on the road to West Hill.

An outing from the Volunteer Inn at Ottery St Mary, pose on the way to Bristol Zoo in 1952. Among those present are: Mr and Mrs Reg Harris, Annette Harris, Millie and Maude Loveless, Stan Symonds, Mrs Hurford, Mrs Reed, Beryl Mansfield and Mary Heale.

Ottery maypole dancers on 1 May 1912, probably in Lord Coleridge's grounds at the Chanter's House.

Left: *Ottery St Mary Infants' School celebrating May Day in 1940.* Left to right, standing: *Peter Harris, Derek Strawbridge, Monica Golesworthy, Gillian Reed, Kathleen Bond;* front row: *Marjorie Paddon, ?, Cyril Reed.*

An outing about to leave the Five Bells Inn in Mill Street, Ottery St Mary, in June 1911 (left). Not much has changed some 40 years later (above) apart from the fact that the window-boxes have gone and the Sidmouth brewers Vallances have acquired the inn, which was demolished in the early 1980s.

Left: *The Swimming Gala, Ottery St Mary, 4 July 1928.*

Right: *Swimmers at Head Weir in 1932. The weir was the site of the old Ottery Swimming Club's Annual Gala, whose secretary at the time was Mr W.H. Bending of 110 Mill Street. Among the 20 events was a 50-yard 'Clothes Race' for men, in which competitors had to wear a coat, trousers and leather boots (or shoes); there was also a 'Top Hat and Umbrella Race' for which competitors had to 'find their own kit'.*

Ottery Day 1909 in Broad Street.

An Ottery Day crowd in 1914, photographed from an upstairs window of the London Hotel.

Market day in Broad Street, 1904.

Above and below: *Sports day at the Chanter's House during the 1907 Ottery Day. The cycle race, just about to start, is obviously a handicap event; the ladies have their own handicap in the egg-and-spoon race in the shape of their voluminous skirts that would make them hard-pressed to hold their own with today's athletes.*

The prizes for the 1909 Ottery Day Sports Meeting.

London-based members of the Old Ottregians meeting in London.

Old Ottregians Society's annual meeting in London, c.1905. Lord Bernard Coleridge (president) is seated centre front next to Sir John Kennaway MP.

The family gathering of Revd William Pryke at the Vicarage on an Ottery Day, c.1905.

Chapter 5

Ottery St Mary at War

In Memoriam

OTTERY ST MARY
1914–18

Pte A. Baker
Pte J. Baker
Cpl W.J. Barrett
Trp A. Bastin
Pte C.D. Bastin
C/Sgt C. Bastone
Flt/Lt S.L. Bennett
Pte A.G. Berry
Pte E.W.H. Berry
Pte F. Bess
Pte W. Board
Pte W.H. Board
Pte A. Bovett
Pte O. Butt
Pte A.F. Butter
Pte J.W. Cann
Pte W.J. Cann
Pte H.T. Churchman
Pte W.C. Churchman
2nd Lieut L.F.R. Coleridge
Pte G. Connett
AB W. Cross
Pte J.T. Cummings
Cpl F.H. Field
Lieut-Col P.C. Gabbet
Pte H. Godfrey
RFN C.W. Hake
AB J. Ham
Pte E. Ham

Pte D.J. Harding
Pte A. Harris
Pte T. Harris
2nd CL/PO I. Hill
Pte E.F. Hooper
Pte H.J. Hooper
L/Cpl W. Howard
1st CL/PO A. Howe
Chief PO G. Howe
Pte W. Howe
Pte W. James
Pte T. Kingdon
Pte R.F. Lee
Pte H. Leatt
Flt Cadet J. Littley
Pioneer A.C. Luxton
Gnr G.H. Luxton
Pte A. Manley
Pte G. Marker
Sgt J. Martin
Pte F.W. Matthews
Cpl J. Melluish
S-Sgt W.H. North
Spr W.J. Palfrey
Pte T.H. Patch
Pte J. Perryman
Pte F. Piney
Pte J. Piney
Pte W.C. Pottinger

Pte P. Pratt
Pte H. Prigg
Pte W.J. Prigg
Of.Stwd F. Richards
RSM E.V. Rooker
Pte H. Salter
CSM J. Salter DCM
Pte S. Salter
Pte W. Sandford
Pte F. Shepperd
AB F.G. Short
Cpl H. Short
Trp W.H. Short
Pte A. Sleete
Pte W.E. Sluggett
Sgt J. Smith
Gnr F.T. Stiling
Pte F. Taylor
Pte W. Thompson
Cpl A. Totterdell
Pte W. Totterdell
Pte F. Tremlett
Pte F. Viney
Pte F.S. Welsman
AB F. White
Sgt G. White MM
Pte F.A. Wilmington
Stoker F. Woodley
Pte W.R. Woodley

1939–45

Leonard Cyril Andrews
Harold Baker
William Cann
Harry Carter
John Franks
Lewis Harding

Samuel Heale
William Lovell
Reginald Maunder
Harry James Perry
Arthur Prigg
Stanley Retter

Frederick Richards
Frank Roberts
Frederick Rowsell
Ronald Stuckey
Gilbert Venner
Reginald Young

ESCOT
1914–18

E. Ham	C.H. Pike	F.A. Wilmington
E.J. Ham	W.J. Prigg	F.C. Flay
D. Harding	L.H. Richards	F. Kingdon
G.F. Hughes	F.T. Stilling	

1939–45

J. Bastin	A. Prigg	Urquart
R. Connett	R. Parsons	

WEST HILL
1914–18

Pte G. Baker	Pte J.T. Cummings	Cpl C.J. Piney
L/Cpl F. Best	P/O J. Hill	Pte H.L. Salter
Pte H. Churchman	Pte W.A. James	Pte W.M. Sandford
Pte W. Churchman	Pte R.T. Lee	Stoker W.H. Thompson

1939–45

Major P.R. Williams	F/S R.W. Hansford	S/Ldr A. Traill
P/O A.C. Hansford	AB E.J. Potter	Lt (RNVR) G.C.A. Hoskins

The First World War, the 'war to end all wars' and the 'Great War' to our forefathers, began for Britain on 4 August 1914 when, in response to Germany's invasion of Belgium, Britain, fulfilling a guarantee that Germany had also undertaken, to go to the defence of that tiny country if it should be threatened, declared war on the invaders.

Panic swept the nation and in Ottery St Mary the football club announced that it would not be fulfilling any fixtures during the present crisis, and *Pulman's Weekly News* reported that sport was not to continue, 'many men had gone to war and there were many men and young lads who should have, and could have, joined the ranks at this critical time.' The football club secretary said he would not act if the league continued in the crisis they were in and endorsed that paper's remarks, which included 'young men would be better employed at the front.' But middle-aged women, middle-aged secretaries and middle-aged editors are never in danger of being called to the Front, of course, and *Pulman's Weekly News* still carried fulsome reports on the local hunts.

The names of the men of Ottery St Mary, Escot and West Hill who made the supreme sacrifice in both world wars 'liveth for ever more' on the memorials of the three Parish Churches concerned. The stark difference in the slaughter on the Western Front during the first conflict and that of the second, is best illustrated by the fact that in Ottery St Mary there are 87 names on the 1914–18 memorial but only 18 on that for 1939–45.

When the Armistice was signed in 1918, the news reached Ottery St Mary by telephone from Exeter and the town almost vanished under a sea of red, white and blue bunting and Union Flags, as well as those of our allies. That evening a gigantic bonfire was lit on Broad Street (which must have brought a few uneasy memories of the 1866 fire to any of the Ottregians of that generation who were present).

The war memorial, St Mary's Church, after its dedication in 1921.

General Sir Henry Redvers Buller who won the VC in 1882 in Zululand and was commander of the British forces for the first part of the Boer War (1899–1902), on a visit to Ottery St Mary, c.1904, in one of the earliest motor cars seen in the town.

First Company, 24th Devonshire Volunteers on manoeuvres at Bulford Camp near Salisbury in 1913. The men are all from Ottery St Mary.

The departure of the Yeomanry from Ottery St Mary on 11 August 1914. How many came back home?

Above and left: *Ottery St Mary's Territorial church parade in 1912.*

In common with many British towns, Ottery St Mary received a German gun after the First World War, which was mounted outside the Town Hall but removed during a Second World War metal salvage drive. Sir John Kennaway, who is standing in front of the gun, handed over the deeds of the Town Hall on 20 July 1958 to Councillor Rutherford, chairman of the UDC. The hall was built by public subscription on land leased by Sir John's great-grandfather and had been covenanted in 1929 to revert to the council for 'the welfare and general convenience of the town of Ottery St Mary.'

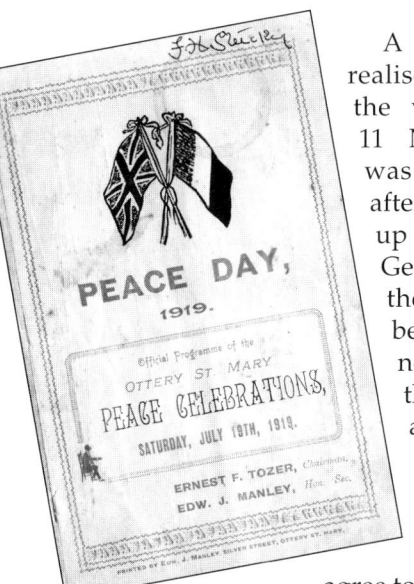

A point not always realised by many is that the war did not end on 11 November 1918, that was merely an armistice after which the Allies drew up their terms for the Germans to accept – and then the war would be officially over. This is not the place to go into the terms of the treaty, although it may be of interest to some to learn that the French included a clause that forced the Germans to agree to stop calling their 'fizzy' wine 'Champagne'. No doubt the French wanted to make sure that the wine opened to celebrate an engagement, a wedding and a christening was the real thing. There is no record of any champagne being drunk during Ottery St Mary's Peace Day celebrations on Saturday 19 July 1919, even at two shillings (10p) a bottle it was well out of the range of most Ottregians, although it is almost certain that many corks were popped at Salston, Cadhay, Escot and elsewhere where two shillings were not so hard to find.

Ernest Tozer, the chairman of the organising committee, had, with Edward Manley, the secretary, prepared a day of merry-making which began with a peal on the bells at St Mary's at six o'clock in the morning, with the bells being rung intermittently throughout the day. At 9.45a.m. the Town Band (always prominent on Ottery's big occasions) paraded through the town with patriotic airs being much to the fore. Sports started at 10a.m. with a 'Walking Race for Men'. The entrants had to complete two laps of the course that began at Broad Street and went via the Monument, Sandhill Street, Chip Lane (now Chapple Lane), Yonder Street, Mill Street as far as the factory and then back to Broad Street. The winner had a handsome prize of ten shillings (50p), the best part of a week's wages at that time. The second man home received five shillings. A slow bicycle race started at Oak Lane and ran to the centre of Broad Street, with the prizes being the same as for the walking race. The ladies, whose walking was one lap of the same course as the men, did not receive any cash prizes – no doubt it was not considered seemly for the genteel sex. Some newer Ottregians may wonder where Oak Lane and the Knapp Field were. Oak Lane is now Pig Lane or Girls School Lane, so named at the time because there was a particularly large oak tree there. There is (was) a Knapp Field at Wiggaton but that is two miles away from Ottery St Mary and the Knapp Field mentioned on the Peace Day programme was in front of the Chanter's House.

Once the walkers had left Broad Street the tables and chairs were put in position for a luncheon which was free to all sailors, soldiers (serving or discharged), volunteers, ringers, bandsmen, etc. No mention is made of how much everyone else paid.

The pageant, that formed up at 1.45p.m. at the railway station, paraded through the town by way of Mill Street, Broad Street, Gold Street and

Peace Thanksgiving Day in Ottery St Mary on 6 July 1919.

Boy Scouts gathering sphagnum moss at Pixies' Parlour during the First World War. The moss was bagged and taken to the Red Cross trains that passed through Sidmouth Junction. It was used for wound dressings.

Below: *Mistakenly called Peace Day on this postcard, pictured is actually the firing of a maroon in The Square at the beginning of the celebrations to mark the Armistice on 11 November 1918.*

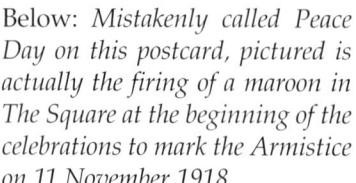

Peace Day was the official end of the First World War and marked the acceptance of the Allied terms by Germany. This postcard, one of many printed at the time, shows the crowd celebrating in Broad Street on 6 July 1919.

Paternoster Row, returned to Sandhill Street, Chip Lane and Yonder Street, then back to Broad Street for dispersal. The tableaux, it almost goes without saying, were of a patriotic nature; St George, Jeanne D'Arc (a sop to our gallant French allies), Britannia, Peace, The Big Four, Empire's Honour and Remember the Heroic Dead. Parading behind the tableaux were the Urban District Council, the Ottery St Mary Town Band, Comrades of the Great War, a Detachment of the 1st Devon Volunteers, VAD Nurses and War Workers, King's School Cadets, Boy Scouts, the fire brigade under Captain M.P. Stuckey, the postmen, the Royal Antediluvian of Buffaloes, the Manchester Unity of Oddfellows and the Rational Friendly Society. If any other Ottregians felt like a stroll they were invited to fall in behind. The comic tableaux followed and in 2004 the two described as 'Golliwogs' and 'Niggers' would be definite non-starters. The first one home in the girls' under-12 race received five shillings (25p and a princely sum to a child at that time).

The evening sports that followed at Chanter's House included a 'Cock Fight in Sacks', a 'Thread-the-Needle' race for ladies and a 'Bun and Ginger Beer' race, in which contestants had to run 50 yards and eat a bun, run another 50 yards and drink a bottle of ginger beer and then spring (or stagger) 50 yards to the finishing line. The 11-strong tug-of-war winners received 33 shillings (15p each).

Dusk was greeted by the firing of several Admiralty flares on the field beside the King's School, Tip Hill, Knapp Field and Ridgeway with a 'huge' bonfire on the Knapp Field.

Tom Paddon

Tom Paddon was born in Tiverton in 1904, one of six children born to Tom and Selina Paddon. On leaving school he started to work half days at the Heathcoat factory before starting work as a labourer on a Templeton farm for a shilling (5p) a week, living in. Agricultural work was not to his liking, however, so he lied about his age and joined the Royal Navy. Once his real age was discovered he went back to farm work. When he was 23 he decided to 'give the Army a go' and joined the Seaforth Highlanders who were recruiting in Exeter and nationwide following the declaration of the First World War.

By this time he had married Elsie Bagwell of Alfington, where his family were living. They had twins, Michael and Monica, but, sadly, Michael died aged just five weeks. Monica survived and moved with her parents to Dover where the Seaforth Highlanders were garrisoned at the castle. There a second daughter, Marjorie, was born and a third daughter was born later in Scotland, called June.

When the Second World War started Tom went to France with the BEF, Elsie and her three daughters

The VE Day street party in Sandhill Street on 8 May 1945.

Ottery St Mary Home Guard in 1940 marching through Broad Street. With men like these waiting for him it is small wonder that Hitler never invaded England.

Ottery St Mary Comrades' first outing on 10 June 1939. They are preparing to leave from the Five Bells in Mill Street. The Five Bells was demolished along with all its neighbours to make room for the new Land of Canaan development scheme.

The 'Welcome Home Party' in Sandhill Street in 1945 for Tom Paddon who had just returned from captivity as a POW.

The 'Welcome Home Party' in 1946 at the Baptist Chapel for Ottery St Mary's men who served in the forces during the Second World War.

Tom Paddon is seen with his wife, Elsie, and two daughters, Marjorie and Monica.

returning to Alphington and moving into a house in Sandhill Street, Ottery St Mary. The Seaforth Highlanders were surrounded at St Valery and Tom was captured and ended up at Stalag 8b, a POW camp in Poland where he spent the rest of the war. When finally freed in May 1945 he came home to Ottery St Mary and the 'Welcome Home' street party. Later that year he started a new career as a rat-catcher, travelling throughout East Devon on a bicycle. Working as a 'rodent operator' for the Devon Agricultural committee he became a master at his art and graduated from his bike to a van. When there was a particularly difficult job to do it was a case of 'send for Tom Paddon'. When the returns were made for his first 18 months his monthly kill never dropped below 1,000 rats. He actually rid one farm of 1,000 in a year.

When the Devon Agricultural committee was wound up he set up on his own and continued to be a scourge to the rats, mice, wasps, hornets and bats until he retired in 1971 aged 71 and moved to Little Close in Winters Lane for a well-earned rest. Both Tom and Elsie were great whist fans and ferried people to outlying 'drives.' Elsie died in 1979 and Tom in 1982.

Tom had been the standard bearer for the Royal British Legion in Ottery St Mary for many years and his daughter remembers the many hours he spent preparing and polishing his boots, gloves and leather standard holster before the Remembrance Day parades and services. In the early 1950s he took the standard to the Albert Hall for the Festival of Remembrance.

The Second World War

Ottery St Mary 'did its bit' during the Second World War, not least by storing parachutes in the Otter Mill factory which was also occupied by the Army. Like almost all British towns and cities Ottery St Mary was well to the forefront when it came to taking part in the

various 'Weeks' organised by the Government to raise cash towards financing the war. No details exist of what the actual target was for the first such 'Week' – War Weapons Week – but Ottery's target was trebled. The target was doubled in Warship Week in 1942, Ottery adopting Motor Torpedo Boat 98, an act that was to lead to a formal exchange of plaques between the town and the ship. Among those present at the ceremony were Captain Ree, the Commander of MTB 98, and Admiral of the Fleet Lord Keyes. At that time a certificate was presented to the town in recognition of its work in raising funds during Tanks for Attack Week – another reward for this was the privilege of naming two tanks.

The town also adopted two Spitfires after Wings for Victory Week in 1943 when, against a target of £60,000, the sum of £100,000 was raised. The logbooks of the two aircraft were held in the council offices. In addition to the two Spitfires the town supplied the Fleet Air Arm with 20 Seafire fighters, the carrier-based version of the Spitfire that had its wings clipped in order that it would fit into the lifts that brought them up from the below-deck hangars to the flight deck.

One proposal that sadly, for the good people of Ottery St Mary at least, did not reach fruition was the arrival of a British Restaurant. There were British Restaurants at neighbouring Sidmouth and Honiton that proved very popular for the cheap and nourishing meals they supplied – a dinner for nine pence (3¾p) and a sweet for three pence (1¼p) and no ration books were required.

The end of hostilities led to the return to London of the evacuees, although a few families did stay and become Ottregians. With the evacuees went the public air-raid shelter in Silver Street that was demolished less than six months after the war ended. In the other direction were the returning POWs who were invited to a welcome home social in the London Hotel.

In 1946 concern was expressed over the intention of the War Office and the Admiralty to acquire training areas in Devon, and the inclusion of part of Harpford Common, an area of great scenic and agricultural value, led to the Parish Council sending a stiff telegram of protest to the Prime Minister (Clement Atlee). Whether it was the telegram that did the trick is not known, but Harpford Common was spared the presence of the military.

The end of the war did not mean the end of rationing and there were shortages in many fields. Coal was the last commodity to be de-rationed in 1954 and even sweets were rationed until 1951 when the personal allowance was one-quarter pound of either sweets or chocolates. Silk was scarce because of the demand for it for the armed forces, especially for parachutes. But it must seem almost archaic that the answer to the shortage was for women to paint their legs in whatever shade of brown suited them. And there was even a black paint if you wanted seams!

Chapter 6

Industries

There has been a grist- and flour-mill on the site of Ottery's factory since the eleventh century, the present building being constructed in 1789–90 at the same time as the factory next door. At first there was an undershot wheel, but it was replaced by an overshot type and used to operate three stones. In order to obtain sufficient power, the millstream was widened and the bed of the River Otter was raised, thus providing enough water for both the mill and the factory. The mill was closed in 1937.

Sir John Duntze and Sir George Yonge, both MPs, had built the factory in an attempt to revive the local wool trade. An 18-foot water-wheel, at the time the largest in England, produced the power for 47 spinning-frames. In 1824 the factory changed from woollen to silk manufacturing and was employing some 400 people.

In 1897 the toilet-brush manufacturers Keetch & Co. bought the factory. Since its opening the factory has been engaged in such diversified activities as bottling mineral water and the making of printing plates, paper bags and clothing.

In 1886 Bernard Drake founded the electrical engineering business of Drake & Gorham at Westminster in London. Immediately after the Second World War the firm acquired a factory at Ottery St Mary, intending to manufacture substantial quantities of a water heater known as the 'Densacone'. Owing to Government restrictions on electricity consumption and the increase in Purchase Tax to 100 per cent in 1948, there was an almost complete cessation of demand in the home market and the manufacture of Bus-Bar Trunking and other electrical components were transferred to Ottery to replace the water-heater production.

In 1954 the name of the firm was changed to Ottermill Switchgear. It was an entirely separate organisation, its only link with Drake & Gorham (Contractors) Ltd being that both companies use the same capital source. In 2004 Ottermill Switchgear products are manufactured under licence in Australia, India and South Africa. Their products can be found in the dome of St Paul's Cathedral, the Bank of England, the first floating oil-drilling rig to be constructed in the UK, most of the South African gold mines, cotton mills in India, Pakistan and Sudan, no less than 11 universities and 20 hospitals in Great

Ottery Brickworks staff in 1928.

Ottery St Mary Brickworks at the foot of Chineway.

Ted Firminger busy working at Ottery Brickworks in 1936.

The workforce at Ottery St Mary Brickworks in 1920.

The Tumbling Weir, known locally as 'The Basin', behind the corn-mill and the factory in 1934. The weir is not, as is often thought, a means of powering either the mill or the factory; it serves as a 'plug hole' and, when neither was working, it carried excess water back to the River Otter.

Workmen cleaning the mill leat at Ottery St Mary in 1918. Notice the ubiquitous cider jar, a necessity for countryside workers at the time.

Left: The bottling factory in 1913 which was owned, at the time, by Mr Colberd.

Above and below: *The tunnel that takes the water from the Tumbling Weir back to the River Otter.*

Corn was ground in this Mill for centuries, the MILL STONES turned by the waters of the SAXON MILL STREAM. IN 1790 this unique TUMBLING WEIR was made to power the new Georgian Serge Factory.

Left: *The sign placed on the wall beside the Tumbling Weir by the East Devon District Council. They were wrong on two counts, however. First, the weir is not unique, several exist on canals in the Midlands; secondly, it does not power anything, being used to return excess water to the river.*

The workforce at Eaton Cutler-Hammer, c.1990.

Above and left: *The end of an era. The final work-force at Eaton Cutler-Hammer before the factory gates closed for the last time in June 2003.*

The Ottermill Switchgear workforce in 1955.

Britain, London Airport, the factories of three major motor car manufacturers, the Downing Street and Treasury reconstruction, Buckfast Abbey and hundreds of other important buildings and plants covering every other major industry in the country.

Closure was threatened for much of the last two decades of the twentieth century and, sadly, the axe fell towards the end of 2003 when the factory was closed.

Otter Nurseries

The year 1963, when the Otter Vale Hatcheries was put up for sale at auction and Malcolm White bought two lots totalling seven acres of grassland, was the birth of Otter Nurseries. The land was ploughed and market-gardening crops were sown – lettuce, cabbage and strawberries – which were sold in the market at Exeter. Soon, greenhouses were erected enabling winter crops to be grown and the scent of freesias prevailed in the house, not for pleasure only, but for grading and bunching for sale to the florist shops in the area.

Market gardening then turned to nursery crops of bedding plants, shrubs, rhododendrons and trees, and from wholesale to retail selling. More land was purchased to make room for fruit and ornamental tree growing and in 2004 there are 100 acres of land growing nursery plants. Around 80 per cent of the plants sold in the Otter Garden Centre are home-grown and this gives a quality control second to none.

The restaurant was opened in the nursery serving home-cooked delicacies that proved very popular, and now a whole day can be spent browsing among the huge range of plants, having a delicious lunch or choosing interesting gifts from the furniture and sundries shop. There are now two other branches, one at Chittleburn Hill in Plymouth, and the other in Babbacombe Road, Torquay. Few would argue with Otter Nurseries' claim on their brochure – 'One of England's largest and finest Garden Centres.' But it is still a family business with many departments, and conservatories and summer-houses, garden machinery, barbecues and furniture all contribute towards making an interesting garden centre – but the plants still remain the primary concern for Malcolm and Marilyn White who are still at the helm in 2004 and enjoying every minute of it.

A fire, probably at the mill-workers' cottage beside the factory, c.1900.

The Ottermill Switch factory from the air, c.1962.

The Corn Mill, Ottery St Mary, c.1940.

Part of the Ottermill Switchgear workforce, c.1960. Left to right, back row: Reg Woolley, Tony Maddon, Ron Whelan, John Andrews, Percy Hill; second row: Toby Diment, Bob Tanner, ?, Geoff 'Nipper' Lee; front row: Arthur Grother, Ern Ebdon, John Taylor.

Ottermill Switchgear with Dick Sharland (left) and Eddie Whitcombe.

Above: Mr Frank Luxton with his workmen rebuilding 'Sitting Bridge' that spans the mill leat, c.1928.

Left: Mrs Marilyn White of Otter Nurseries arranging plants in the indoor section.

An aerial view of Otter Nurseries taken soon after it opened in 1963. In 2004 all the land on the top side of Gosford Road has been incorporated in the nursery.

The opening of the first retail greenhouse-plant shop by the well-known BBC gardening expert Percy Thrower (left), with Marilyn and Malcolm White.

Otter Nurseries in winter.

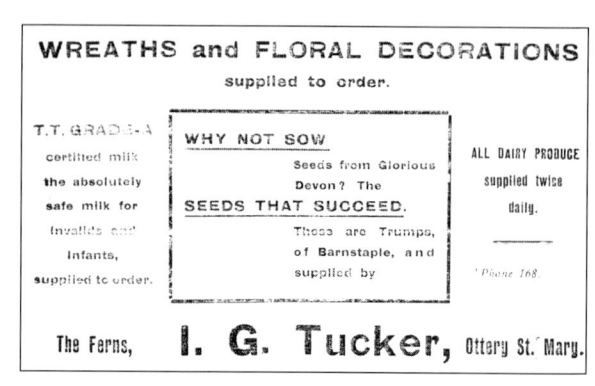

Shops and Streets

The East Devon Motor Company, Mill Street, Ottery St Mary in 1927. The tall man in the entrance is Henry John Lee, the proprietor. In 2004 it is Down's Motors who run the well-known local Otter coaches from there.

The King's Arms Hotel on the corner of Sandhill Street and Gold Street, c.1910.

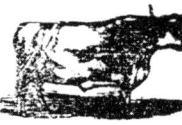

- VENNER, -
FAMILY BUTCHER,

All Meat of the best quality only.

Families waited on daily for Orders.

OTTERY ST. MARY.

Telephone 17.

Tip Hill, Ottery St Mary, c.1903.

Above: *Heath's ironmongery store in Mill Street, Ottery St Mary, in the 1920s. Later Freddy Mayne bought the business. In 2004 it is the premises of John Williams who runs it as a television and electrical shop.*

Bradley End, Tip Hill, Ottery St Mary, c.1910. Later it became the home of the sisters of the Marist Convent School. The town fire-engine was housed at the top of the bank on the left (the entrance to Longdogs Lane).

The London Hotel, Gold Street, Ottery St Mary, c.1949.

The East Devon Hunt meets in Broad Street, Ottery St Mary in 1919.

Mr F. Heath's shop in Mill Street, c.1908, the site of John Williams' TV and radio shop in 2004.

Mill Street, Ottery St Mary, c.1960. The white building in the background is the now-demolished Five Bells Inn.

Chineway Road, Ottery St Mary, in 1968 before the Leaman estate was built. Prices on the new estate ranged from £3,250 for a two-bedroom semi-detached bungalow and up to £5,000 for a four-bedroom detached chalet bungalow.

Sheep pens at Ottery St Mary market in Paternoster Row in 1909. The police station (with the porch) has moved to The Flexton. The market moved to a permanent site that was near the railway station, c.1912. It was closed around the end of the 1950s.

Right and below: *Market day in The Square in 1923.*

Above: *Charles Lovell's cycle shop in Jesu Street with an impressive display of bicycles outside on the pavement. The premises later became the Scala until 1942 when it was damaged by fire. When it reopened later that year its name was changed to The Cinema until it was closed around 1954; in 2004 it is Morris' carpet shop. The town of Ottery St Mary has been scoured for a picture of the old cinema without success – the nearest we can come up with is a programme for May 1950 (right) which, to an older generation of Ottregians, brings back nostalgic memories of the golden age of the cinema with such names as Michael Wilding, Larry Parkes, Anna Neagle, Vivien Leigh and Ralph Richardson.*

Above: *Silver Street, Ottery St Mary, c.1908. The Devon and Cornwall Bank is now Lloyds Bank and Manley's newsagents' shop on the left has been demolished. The site is now occupied by the National Westminster Bank.*

Right: *The King's Arms Hotel, Gold Street, c.1910.*

Right: *Charlie Burdett behind the counter in Trumps' Stores (now the Victoria Wine Shop), Ottery St Mary in the 1950s. Obviously an Oxydol promotion is taking place.*

Below: *Mill Street, Ottery St Mary, c.1910. The metal poles on the left were for tying the sun-blinds on, although it was not unknown for customers to hitch their horses to them.*

Yonder Street, Ottery St Mary, c.1905.

New Street, Ottery St Mary, c.1905.

Victoria Terrace, Ottery St Mary, c.1910.

Ottery St Mary's cottage hospital, c.1913. Mrs Isabella Elliott originally gave it to the people of Ottery St Mary but in 2004 it is being converted into five luxury flats.

Lamb Court, Ottery St Mary, c.1910.

The staff at the Ottery St Mary branch of the local Co-operative Society, c.1914. The sign saying that it is Branch No. 6 suggests that there were at least five other such shops in the area.

Mr Hine and his family outside his grocery shop in Paternoster Row, Ottery St Mary, c.1914.

Above: *Looking down into Silver Street from Gold Street, c.1920.*

Mr Moore's shoe shop in Jesu Street, c.1936. It became the Toy and Candy Shop (below) run by Les Carter. Around the start of the twenty-first century it was converted into a private dwelling.

In the 1960s almost all the young bloods of the town (or any town come to that) had a motorcycle. Broad Street, outside of Roberts' and Lovell's shops, was a popular meeting place for Ottery's 'bikers.' Left to right: Toby Hawkins, Humphrey Collins, Jim Isaac, Ron Rowland, Peter Bull, Tom Gush, Tony Carter, John Lear.

Right and below: Before and after. Demolition work on the Plume of Feathers in Yonder Street in 1994 and the housing that replaced it.

The Mason's Arms in Sandhill Street, c.1999, shortly before it closed.

Digby Cottage in Hind Street.

Once the town was lit entirely by gas and, although electricity has long-since taken over, one of the old gas-lamp brackets can still be found in Saddlers Lane in 2004.

87

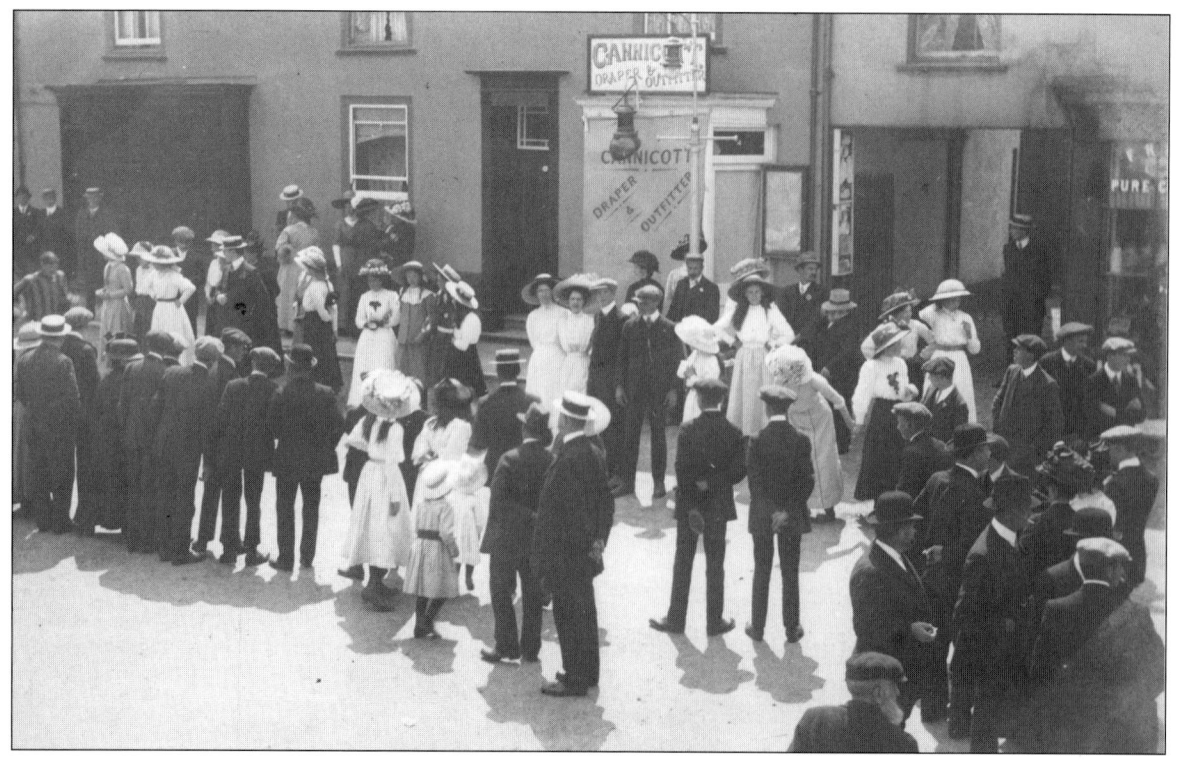

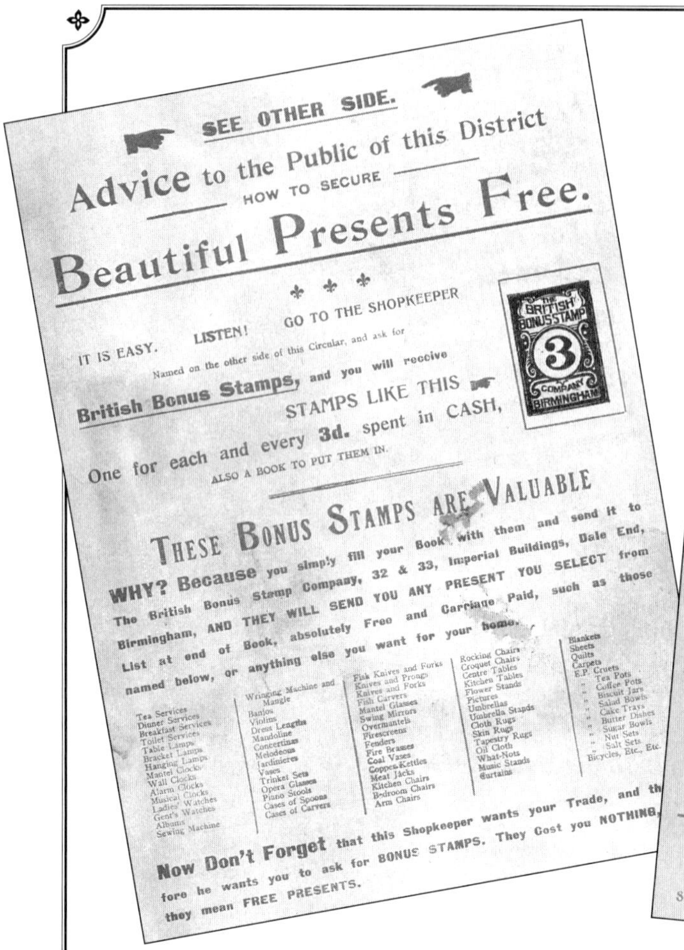
SEE OTHER SIDE.
Advice to the Public of this District
HOW TO SECURE
Beautiful Presents Free.
IT IS EASY. LISTEN! GO TO THE SHOPKEEPER
Named on the other side of this Circular, and ask for
British Bonus Stamps, and you will receive
STAMPS LIKE THIS
One for each and every 3d. spent in CASH,
ALSO A BOOK TO PUT THEM IN.
THE BRITISH BONUS STAMP 3 COMPANY BIRMINGHAM
THESE BONUS STAMPS ARE VALUABLE
WHY? Because you simply fill your Book with them and send it to The British Bonus Stamp Company, 32 & 33, Imperial Buildings, Dale End, Birmingham, AND THEY WILL SEND YOU ANY PRESENT YOU SELECT from List at end of Book, absolutely Free and Carriage Paid, such as those named below, or anything else you want for your home.
Tea Services, Dinner Services, Breakfast Services, Toilet Services, Table Lamps, Bracket Lamps, Hanging Lamps, Mantel Clocks, Wall Clocks, Alarm Clocks, Musical Clocks, Ladies' Watches, Gent's Watches, Albums, Sewing Machine
Wringing Machine and Mangle, Banjos, Violins, Dress Lengths, Mandoline, Concertinas, Melodeons, Jardinieres, Vases, Trinket Sets, Opera Glasses, Piano Stools, Cases of Spoons, Cases of Carvers
Fish Knives and Forks, Knives and Prongs, Knives and Forks, Fish Carvers, Mantel Glasses, Swing Mirrors, Overmantels, Firescreens, Fenders, Fire Brasses, Coal Vases, Copper Kettles, Meat Jacks, Kitchen Chairs, Bedroom Chairs, Arm Chairs
Rocking Chairs, Croquet Chairs, Centre Tables, Kitchen Tables, Flower Stands, Pictures, Umbrellas, Umbrella Stands, Cloth Rugs, Skin Rugs, Tapestry Rugs, Oil Cloth, What-Nots, Music Stands, Curtains
Blankets, Sheets, Quilts, Carpets, E.P. Cruets, " Tea Pots, " Coffee Pots, " Biscuit Jars, " Salad Bowls, " Cake Trays, " Butter Dishes, " Sugar Bowls, " Nut Sets, " Salt Sets, Bicycles, Etc., Etc.
Now Don't Forget that this Shopkeeper wants your Trade, and therefore he wants you to ask for BONUS STAMPS. They Cost you NOTHING, they mean FREE PRESENTS.

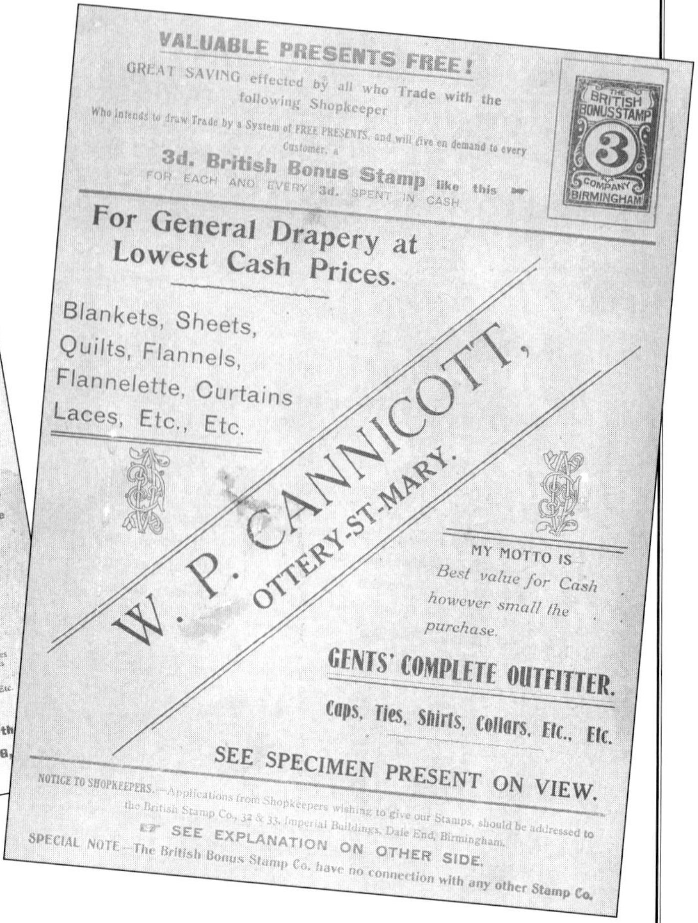
VALUABLE PRESENTS FREE!
GREAT SAVING effected by all who Trade with the following Shopkeeper
Who intends to draw Trade by a System of FREE PRESENTS, and will give on demand to every Customer, a
3d. British Bonus Stamp like this
FOR EACH AND EVERY 3d. SPENT IN CASH
THE BRITISH BONUS STAMP 3 COMPANY BIRMINGHAM
For General Drapery at Lowest Cash Prices.
Blankets, Sheets, Quilts, Flannels, Flannelette, Curtains Laces, Etc., Etc.
W. P. CANNICOTT,
OTTERY-ST-MARY.
MY MOTTO IS
Best value for Cash however small the purchase.
GENTS' COMPLETE OUTFITTER.
Caps, Ties, Shirts, Collars, Etc., Etc.
SEE SPECIMEN PRESENT ON VIEW.
NOTICE TO SHOPKEEPERS.—Applications from Shopkeepers wishing to give our Stamps, should be addressed to the British Stamp Co., 32 & 33, Imperial Buildings, Dale End, Birmingham.
SEE EXPLANATION ON OTHER SIDE.
SPECIAL NOTE—The British Bonus Stamp Co. have no connection with any other Stamp Co.

W.P. Cannicott, a draper in Broad Street, obviously ran a 1920s version of the more recent Greenshield Stamps bonus scheme. The shop, pictured here on an Edwardian Ottery Day, is the Country Farm Butcher's shop in 2004.

CANNICOTT DRAPER & OUTFITTER
CANNICOTT DRAPER & OUTFITTER

The Brock family ran a confectionary and tobacconist shop in Mill Street for 90 years, taking over from Mrs Hindom in 1906. In 1996 it became Otter Gems, a jewellery business. In the picture from around 1908 Mr Brock is seen with her two daughters Gladys (left), later Mrs Grange, and Doris, later Mrs Selley.

Mrs Hindom pictured outside the family confectionary and stationery business in Mill Street, c.1900.

Below: *Looking into Silver Street from The Square, c.1910, with Huxtable & Streat's shoe shop on the left. Slee's Bazaar on the right was mainly a tobacconist shop with some stationery lines as well.*

The Plume of Feathers Inn, Yonder Street, c.1905, when the land-lord was a Mr Williams as indicated by the inn's signboard. At the time the housing in Yonder Street only went as far as Slade Road but, of course, the trees and fields in the background have now been swallowed up by development.

The Ottery St Mary branch of the local Co-operative Society in Yonder Street in 1907 which is still in existence on the same site, albeit with a modern shop front. The wheelbarrow outside is the Edwardian equivalent of the more modern errand boy's carrier bicycle.

The staff of Trump's Stores outside the shop in Broad Street, in Ottery St Mary, during the early 1920s. Among those pictured are: *Mr Young* (driver of the pony trap), *Stan Isaac* (van driver), *Mr Ford* (white coat), *Mr Temple and Mr White* (manager), *Miss Fry* (by the door), *Mr Rudge* (motorcycle) *and Charlie Burdett. The motorcycle delivered groceries as far away as Payhembury and Buckerell.*

Broad Street, Ottery St Mary, in the 1950s when the Volunteer Inn's sign (on the right) *showed that it still belonged to the now-closed Vallance's Brewery at Sidmouth.*

Left: *Regulars at the Volunteer Inn take time off from enjoying their pints to have their picture taken in the 1950s. Among those pictured are: Jim Pearcy, Len Russell, Mrs Streat (landlady), John Oxenham, Ralph Streat, Jess Pike, Donald Baker, Mr Sandicott, Mr Turner and Ray Baker.*

Right: *Reg Harris, the Ottery St Mary baker, beside his 1¼ litre 1939 MG and outside his Broad Street shop in 1952.*

Left: *Charles Lovell's Central Garage in Brook Street in the 1960s. Formerly in Broad Street, it retained its Central Garage name after its move in 1973 when it was no longer in the centre of the town.*

Right: One of the few remaining yellow AA town or village signs that sprang up all over the country between the two world wars. They always gave the mileage to London which from Wiggaton, a small hamlet south of Ottery St Mary, was 156¼ miles.

J. H. PRIGG,

CARRIER, GENERAL HAULAGE,
-AND FURNITURE REMOVER,-

JESMOND, RIDGEWAY, OTTERY ST. MARY.
('Phone : 38).

LEAVING BROAD STREET FOR EXETER AT 9.15, AND
LEAVING WHITE HART SOUTH STREET, EXETER AT 4.

TUESDAYS AND FRIDAYS.

ANY COMMISSION UNDERTAKEN
NOTHING TOO SMALL--NOTHING TOO BIG

Brook Cottage (right) at Wiggaton, a tiny hamlet to the south of Ottery St Mary on the Sidmouth road. Floods destroyed it in 1962.

LEAMAN HOMES

OTTERY ST. MARY DEVELOPMENT

Freehold prices

which are completely inclusive of all road charges, full oil fired central heating and hot water system, brick built garages, etc.

Two bedroom "Creedy" semi-detached bungalow	£3,250
Two Bedroom detached bungalows	£3,650
Three Bedroom "Culm" semi-detached houses	£3,250
Three Bedroom "Creedy" semi-detached bungalow	£3,800
Three Bedroom detached bungalows	£4,450
Four Bedroom detached "Lowman" chalet bungalows	£5,000

Of the above prices, in the case of the two bedroom bungalows, three bedroom semi-detached houses and three bedroom semi-detached bungalows, £850 relates to the cost of the ground and in the case of the three bedroom detached bungalows and the four bedroom chalet bungalows £950, and the remainder is the price of the property to be erected.

On signing the contract a deposit of 10 per cent of the value of the plot is required and the remaining 90 per cent is due on completion of the purchase of same. The cost of the property itself is payable when certain stages are reached in its construction. This method of payment has been adopted as it is found most convenient for purchasers and does enable prices to be kept to a minimum.

Mr and Mrs Fred Baker ran a greengrocer's business in Silver Street, seen here on the left in the 1920s. Much of the produce sold in the shop came from their market garden in Hind Street (now the car park).

Ottery St Mary grocer F.H. Shepperd's delivery van outside his shop in Silver Street, c.1929. Bill Pearcy on the left.

Francis Henry Shepperd with a member of his staff outside his shop in Silver Street, Ottery St Mary in 1902. The house and shop were built in c.1818 by Thomas Shepperd, Francis Shepperd's grandfather, who is listed in Pigot's 1844 Directory of Devon as a grocer, tea dealer, linen and woollen draper and wine and spirit merchant.

Chapter 7

Disasters

Ottery St Mary's position at the foot of a steep range of hills, down which streams and even ditches become raging torrents when heavy storms sweep the area, has always made it prone to flooding. Perhaps no more so than in 1997 when the heaviest cloudburst in living memory had its epicentre over the town, the resulting disastrous flood causing thousands of pounds worth of damage and untold human misery. There had been much early flooding including, in October 1960, 'a significant flood' that brought insurance claims amounting to over £3,000 from the public, a significant amount at the time. At the time of writing (February 2004) yet another cloudburst has sent water flooding through the town at a time when work on a Flood Prevention Scheme is under way.

But it is not always water that has turned the town into a disaster zone – sometimes it was the lack of water, such as on 25 May 1866, when a fire that broke out in Yonder Street at around midday spread its way through the town and turned a large part of it into a heap of smouldering ruins. The fire had started in the rear of the premises of the Charity School in Yonder Street which was soon in flames and, with a strong wind fanning the blaze, it quickly spread down the street towards the Red Lion Inn which was burning fiercely less than an hour after the alarm had been raised. Mrs Burrows, the landlady, barely had time to drag the contents of the inn to safety before the fire reached her. However, before the fire had reached the inn all three of the town's fire-engines were on the spot, but at first some difficulty was experienced in obtaining a sufficient supply of water. This was a problem that dogged the firemen's footsteps throughout the day unless they were close to a large enough stream to serve their pumps for any length of time. It was, of course, the age of the hand pump which

Kidney Bean Square off Sandhill Street, Ottery St Mary, in 1960 when two of the fronts of the five cob-built houses collapsed. The five houses were demolished at the time and two semi-detached houses replaced them.

A steamroller lost its front roller when navigating Gold Street on 30 June 1930. The girl on the extreme right is Nora Tolman (later Mrs Hart).

Firemen fighting the blaze that destroyed six thatched cottages in North Street, Ottery St Mary, in 1905.

The Alidair Viscount aircraft that crash-landed at Bishops Court Farm, Ottery St Mary, after running out of fuel just before reaching its Exeter destination. It was on its return flight from Santander in Spain. There were no casualties among the 58 passengers or the four crew members, but four of Mr Carter's sheep were killed whilst grazing in the field.

A Regent petrol tanker lost is brakes negotiating Silver Street in 1937 and ended up crashing backwards into the London Hotel.

The Furze Brook, Ottery St Mary, on the evening of the 1997 flood that swamped most of the town centre after torrential rain swept off the saturated fields on Chineway and down into the town.

Right and below: The aftermath of the 1997 flooding of Ottery St Mary's town centre.

Jesu Street after the fire of 1866.

Mill Street after the fire of 1866.

became very hard work after even an hour – Ottery's fire raged for seven hours.

Other victims were Mrs Burrows' neighbours, Mr Channon, a grocer, and another Mr Channon who was a plumber. When the fire spread up Tip Hill on the Sidmouth Road all but one of the 16 houses there were destroyed. The occupants included Mr Hearen, the veterinary surgeon, Mr Benden, a shoemaker, and Mr Tremlet who was a tailor.

The fire was well out of control and headed into the centre of the town, spreading down Mill Street towards Mr Colin Newberry's silk factory. On its way it destroyed, among others, the houses of Mr Benden, another shoemaker, Mr Winover, a harness maker, and Mr Pike who was a bacon factor. When the fire reached the home of local solicitor Mr Davey, it had to spread across his large garden to reach the house, which it did with comparative ease. The flames went quickly behind the line of the dwellings, destroying the butcher Digby's home, Mr Salter's butcher shop, Mr Salter's grocery business, the Volunteer Inn (Mr Hambling), and the houses of Mr Green, Mr Hutchings and also Mr Goldberry, who was also a shoemaker. It swept on along Mill Street and, in the end, had destroyed between 60 and 70 houses there, some of them new buildings which had been solidly constructed of bricks with slate roofs rather than thatch, which was the cause of many a town-centre fire in eighteenth- and nineteenth-century England. Ottery St Mary itself had also been devastated by fire almost exactly 100 years earlier.

Once the size of the conflagration was realised, an appeal for help had been wired to Exeter. But it was four o'clock before the first engine, the 'West of England', arrived. Hard on its heels was the 'Royal' which had taken only an hour and nine minutes to make the journey, very good going at the time over roads that would have been rutted dust bowls in summer and mud-baths after rain. The 'Norwich' came a close third soon afterwards. All three fire-engines, as their names suggest, belonged to insurance companies.

By this time (five o'clock) the flames had almost reached the walls of the silk factory after consuming most of the houses on the left-hand side of the street.

Although it looks more like a German city in 1945, this is a picture of Tip Hill after the great fire of Ottery St Mary in 1866.

Ottery St Mary with just a couple of days to go before Bonfire Night in 2001.

The London Hotel in Gold Street after a disastrous fire there in 1982.

The one exception was the Weslyan Chapel that escaped with a scorching. The more church-going generation of Ottregians put this down as a sign from above. Just when it seemed that the fire was coming under control, the wind veered in a completely different direction and crossed the road to burn the home of Mr Huxtable (another shoemaker) completely to the ground before consuming much of Mr Fowell's large corn-mills, where the fire was finally stopped around 7.30 when the fire brigades and town's inhabitants pulled down some buildings in its path.

The fire was still raging elsewhere and most of the furniture from the houses in danger had been dragged out into the middle of the street for safety. Even there it was still in danger from sparks and embers of spitting woodwork. When the fire had been at its height, it was so hot that the firemen could hardly do their duty. Happily there were no fatalities, but several people, especially the firemen, suffered scorched faces and sore eyes. One elderly woman of 92 refused to leave her house until the flames had burnt most of the roof off – and then they almost had to drag her out.

Speculation was rife as to the cause of the fire. Most fingers of suspicion fell on a woman who had vacated a cottage close to the rear of the Charity School the day before and burnt a considerable amount of paper and rubbish in the fireplace. The fire was thought to have ignited the soot in the chimney that smouldered during the night before burning its way through the woodwork into the school.

The following day a dazed town took stock of a scene that looked like many Germany cities would nearly 80 years later after the attentions of the RAF during the Second World War. Mr Baker, the overseer, needed a map to count the correct number of buildings that had gone. With the aid of Mr Digby, a builder, he came up with 111; many of them were inhabited by more than one family and well over 700 people had been rendered homeless by the fire, 300 of them, being poor people, were destitute as well and would have to depend upon the charity of their neighbours – so much so that the small houses that had escaped the fire and taken in the homeless were badly overcrowded and there were fears of an outbreak of fever unless the people of the surrounding countryside came to the rescue.

Fred Stuckey with Ottery St Mary's Fire Brigade's 1911 manual fire pump.

A caravan on the cricket field after the flood of 1968.

Ottery St Mary Fire Brigade in 1950. Left to right, back row: *Charles Turner, Frank Down, Tom Bishenden, Bill Berry;* front row: *Jack Rowland, Bill Manley, Charles Ash.*

The 1932 wedding of Mr and Mrs Reg Keitch who are leaving for their reception in Ottery St Mary's fire-engine. Sir John Kennaway is by the bonnet with firemen Arthur Sparkes, George Isaac, Frank Dyer, Harry Stuckey, Jack Coles and Bill Hanford in support.

Ottery St Mary Fire Brigade, 1889. Left to right, back row: H. Gover, Tom Dyer senr, deputy captain George Channon, captain J.H. Newton, R. Banfield, E. 'Knocker' Stocker, C. Salter. The other names are unknown.

The hose handcart belonging to Ottery St Mary Fire Brigade, c.1905.

Sub-captain Billy Handford, Ottery St Mary Fire Brigade, 1932.

An old Ottery St Mary fire-engine from the 1890s.

Chapter 8

Local Government

The Ottery St Mary Council came into being in 1894 when it consisted of nine members with Mr Squire combining the duties of surveyor, town clerk and treasurer, and a Mr Tolman was the road sweeper, a much more laborious task than today because he had to contend with unmade streets. During the winter he would constantly sweep and maintain clean crossing paths at strategic positions around the town.

Although the workings of the Ottery St Mary Urban District Council, if not complete, are fairly extensive (in newspaper-cutting form) for the periods 1932–62 and 1973–4, no such notes exist of the workings of the Ottery Town Council since it was formed following the reorganisation of local government in 1974.

The first cutting is dated October 1932 when Mr W.F. Thomas, a local solicitor, was the clerk to the council, a position he held from 1913–40. He came to the town from South Africa c.1906 and, retiring in 1940 because of ill health, he died in 1946. His successor was Mr S.V. Mossop. Mr Thomas' lengthy service of 27 years was dwarfed, however, by Mr T.J. Whicker, the deputy clerk who was appointed when the Urban District Council was established under the Local Government Act of 1894 and served for 48 years until his retirement in 1942. His was a full-time appointment that saw him serve under the part-time clerks. During the First World War, when the surveyor was serving in the Army, Mr Whicker carried out his duties as well. The first chairman of the new council in 1894 was Revd Read, the vicar of Alfington, who topped the poll and was one of nine members elected from 20 candidates.

In 1942 the council consisted of the following: R.J. Copp, chairman; W.M. Stuckey, vice-chairman; A.G. Palfrey, senior councillor; and Messrs I.G. Tucker, J. Salter and J.H. Mace among others.

Ottery Town Council's road workforce in 1922.

Roadworks in Hind Street opposite Piccadilly Lane, Ottery St Mary, c.1930.

One of the most pressing priorities facing the council, even before the end of the war (8 May 1945) was the provision of badly needed council-housing. For this purpose around 8^1/$_2$ acres of land at Winters Lane and another 4^1/$_2$ at Spring Gardens were purchased in March 1945 and a tender for the erection of 26 houses costing £31,876 was accepted on 6 February 1947. Further schemes at Longdogs Lane and West Hill were submitted to the Ministry of Health for approval and, in March 1948, Ottery's first postwar council estates were opened at Spring Gardens and Alfington – 38 houses in all.

It was around that time (May 1947) that the possibility of a merger between Honiton Borough and Rural Councils and the Ottery St Mary Urban District Council was suggested following the first annual report of the Local Government Boundary Commission. The threat would meander on for some years but, in the end, Honiton and Ottery remained separate until both became part of the East Devon District Council in 1974. The two towns did unite in an attempt to prevent further mass water extraction from the River Otter by Taunton Town Council, although Honiton Town Council did most of the opposing. In 1949 Taunton wanted another 100,000,000 gallons but, after discussion, they were only allowed to draw water from the River Otter when it was in flood. It was a time of drought with prayers for rain in West Country in September, and the Ottery St Mary Fly-Fishing Club joined in the battle over Taunton's wishes for more and more water – the River Otter was a well-known trout stream.

It was in 1949 that an advertisement appeared in *Pulman's Weekly News* inviting tenders for one horse in excellent condition and one cart in sound condition. Was it only half a century ago that a horse pulled the dust car?

During the 1950s more and more council-housing was provided and, by 21 June 1957, the number of such houses had gone up from 48 in 1945 (at the end of the Second World War) to 221, and there were still more in the pipeline. Of particular concern was the need to house workers in expanding local industry, particularly Ottermill Switchgear. This brought accusations (unfounded) that to qualify for a council-house one had to work at the factory, accusations that were swiftly refuted by the council chairman, Mr G.R. Rutherford.

Almost every town in England has seen one of its streets newly-laid and almost immediately dug up by one of the utilities for either pipe or cable laying. Ottery St Mary's Mill Street was relaid in 1959, dug up in October 1960 by the Post Office for cable laying, and then again six months later when more roadworks were carried out. The three weeks of disruption proved to be the final straw for the normally-placid population and a rash of placards broke out, renaming the area as 'Dusty Creek'. Raleigh House became the 'Dust Bowl Hotel'.

It has to be either the efficiency of the Urban District Council or the good spirit of the Ottregians, we suspect the latter, that the clerk was able to report to the council in 1958 that, for the fifteenth successive year, there were no rent arrears.

Work near the slipway that would leave the new A30 trunk road for Ottery St Mary at Daisy Mount, and the completed controversial A30 road that local protestors claimed was 'the noisiest road in Britain'. The reason for the heavy traffic heading out of the West Country is that it was taken on the day after the 1998 total eclipse of the sun, for which many people travelled to Cornwall.

Widening the B3174 road at its junction with the road to Otter Nurseries and Gosford. The name on the steamroller is that of Fothergill Brothers who, presumably, are doing the work in the early 1920s.

Work on the B3174's junction with the new dual carriageway on the A30, part of the Folkstone–Exeter trunk road, in 1997.

Sarcastic placards in Mill Street in 1959 when the road was dug up for the second time in six months, causing three weeks of disruption to the locals.

Chapter 9

Ottery St Mary's Census Returns
and the Town's Health

Census Returns

1811	2,880
1821	3,522
1831	3,849
1441	4,194
1851	4,421
1861	4,340
1871	4,110
1881	3,973
1891	3,855
1901	3,495
1911	3,699
1921	3,538
1931	3,713
1941	no census
1951	4,015
1961	4,121
1971	5,834
1981	7,069
1991	7,417

Although the population of Ottery St Mary had slightly more than doubled in the twentieth century, the major part of that increase was since the 1960s when it rose by 3,294. This was an increase due in no small way to the drift away from the inner cities into the country, and also the increased longevity brought about by more and more modern medicines. Amazingly, between 1961–71, there were as many as 1,711 new Ottregians. The stark contrast is that the population fell by 845 during the last 40 years of the nineteenth century.

The only decrease during the twentieth century came at the end of the second decade when the combination of the slaughter during 1914–18 and the flu epidemic that followed in 1919 (which is said to have killed some 29 million people throughout the world) would have been two contributory factors.

Life was far shorter 150 years ago and the reasons are hardly hidden away in the Report to the Board of Health by Thomas Rammell, the superintending inspector, in 1850. A total of 112 members of the public had become worried that the town was suffering repeated epidemics of various fevers and that the

4,000 people in Ottery St Mary were said to have a life expectancy of only 24 years – which would have been hard to accept.

The eight miles of roads in the parish were under the care of four unpaid way wardens; three of them were farmers and the soil to make the roads was dug out of the river. Two and a half miles of the road were in the middle (the town), 'being in such a dilapidated state that much of the transport passing though the town needed an extra horse to navigate the soft and dirty streets.' The report goes on to describe in some detail the unhealthy conditions in the town, mentioning the non-existence of drainage, human waste being heaped up outside the houses or thrown into pits, much of it finding its way into the local streams that were the only source of drinking-water for many households. The gutters were not covered and this, along with the piles of waste, must have been quite unpleasant during the summer. The only attempt to remove the manure piles came from the town scavenger, who then compounded the folly in larger piles, still around the town, where it was left to decompose before being sold for manure at five shillings (25p) for two cart-loads. The scavenger was said to be unpaid but it was hardly a labour of love because he did get the five shillings at the end.

The number of privies, or rather the lack of them, was dreadful – even the British and Foreign School in Batts Lane only had two for 91 pupils. The school was in close proximity to Chapple and Jesu Street where, including Batts Lane, there were 228 houses and 58 pigsties and cowsheds, all with their waste emptying into two open pits or yards from where it frequently was washed by rain into the gutters. The two privies at the school were placed over open pits and they emptied directly into the brook.

Some financial help was at hand. There were several charities doling out money and goods, such as blankets or food, to the poorer inhabitants of the town. One such charity was the Ottery Feoffees Charity or the Somersetshire Trust, which arose from the gift of Henry Beaumont, who by his will of 17 March 1590 left £800 for the purchase of land for the poor of Ottery St Mary, providing five pounds a year for ever, and made his wife, Elizabeth, sole executrix of his will. Elizabeth Beaumont appointed 12 trustees, who had to be inhabitants of Ottery St Mary. The will stated that any trustees who resided outside the parish for any period of six months would cease to hold office. There is still a Beaumont House in the town on Ridgeway. The trustees had to let the property by public auction after one month's public notice at the best annual rent reasonably obtainable. There were various properties, the rents of most going to several charities. The rent for the land at Waxway, for instance, was to be distributed by the trustees in sums not exceeding 20 shillings (£1) each among the oldest labouring men of the parish not receiving parochial relief. The rents of Laver Ash Meadow were given in the same way.

Other properties included a dwelling-house, shop and premises in Silver Street let to John Edward Baker in 1901 at a rent of £25 per year; and another dwelling-house with courtelage, outbuildings and gardens in Yonder Street with two orchards and a close of arable land at the rear, for which Thomas Dyer paid a rent of £20. The Parish Council rented one property, an engine house in Silver Street, presumably used for pumping water, at a rental of one pound. The council also paid £9.19s.6d. rent for a close of arable land called Four Acres near Shutes – tradition has it that the land was used for their horses. In all there were 27 properties held by the trust including four almshouses in Yonder Street and three in Sandhill Street. In 2004 the Yonder Street almshouses are known as Sherman House and are still let at very low rents to appropriate tenants. The three houses in Sandhill Street were demolished and rebuilt as four flats known as Robert Hone House and also let at low rents.

The blacksmith's shop in Yonder Street, rented by John Streat in 1901 at £18.18s.0d. per year, would, one day, have Ottery St Mary's Co-op shop as a neighbour.

Although now a private residence, it can still be seen in the town in 2004.

Quite a large sum (around £2,500) was raised by the Feoffees when they sold 14 of their properties. The biggest sum (£620) was for 21 acres of land known as Leggeshayes, a name no longer to be found in Ottery St Mary. Two cottages in garden ground at Burnt House were sold for £48.12s.3d. in 1890 – presumably Burnt House Farm on the Gosford Road just beyond Otter Nurseries, although there is no tradition of any fire at that place.

Immediately after the great fire of 1866 a committee was formed for the purpose of collecting funds and administering to persons in need of immediate relief, such as food, clothing, bedding, shelter and tools, and for applying to the authorities to enforce sanitary measures. This committee was directed to consider provisions for schools. A statement of accounts was issued to all subscribers to a fund in September 1866 that showed that a total of £3,403.18s.4d. had been raised, and there remained in hand the sum of £1,126.13s.5d. The committee sought the opinions of the subscribers as to how they should dispose of that balance, and they suggested that £800 should be used towards building the new boys' school (Yonder Street) and the new girls' school (Sandhill Street), for which sites had been provided, and the remainder to be applied to the relief of the poor of the parish in case of another disaster, whether fire or disease. It was also suggested that one of two other things could also be done with regard to any future conflagration. The first was the gift of a fire-engine and ancillary appliances and their maintenance for the parish, or the support of a voluntary fire brigade. The second was a water tank, but this idea fell through.

Chapter 10

Sport

Ottery St Mary Cricket Club

The Ottery St Mary Cricket Club is the second-oldest club in East Devon after Sidmouth, who were founded in 1823, Ottery being formed in June 1858, Axminster in 1874 and Seaton in 1875, although a Seaton club had briefly flourished between 1870–73, and Budleigh Salterton in 1930. Ottery's first meetings were held at the Red Lion Inn that was situated at the corner of Tip Hill and Jesu Street. John Whitham in his *History of Ottery St Mary* tells us that a month after the foundation of the club the secretary wrote to the Exeter club saying that Ottery St Mary was 'desirous of playing a match if you are desirous of accepting a challenge from us.' There are records of various matches including one

against Exmouth who scored 109 and dismissed Ottery for 49 and 38 and won by an innings and 22 runs. Early home games were played at Cadhay.

Unfortunately records are not to hand of the exploits of the club's early days. A programme exists for a concert held for the benefit of club funds in the 1920s and the names of the participants include such well-known Ottery St Mary names as Stuckey and Manley. In 1909 Ottery St Mary were bowled out for 40 at Honiton on the old pitch, thought to have been in the field behind the Copper Castle toll-house, with Hussey taking 8–12. Earlier, Honiton had made 143–4.

The club took on a new impetus shortly after the Second World War, namely at the instigation of the then town clerk, Bill Bennett, and an influx

Ottery St Mary Cricket Club's annual dinner in 1950.

Ottery St Mary Cricket Club, 1958. Left to right: Fred Burns, Jay Mewse, Peter Bond, Donald Finnegan, Stan Baker, John Harvey, Jack Retter, Henry Lawrence, Charles Lamb, Ray Pollard, Laurie Spencer, Harry Channon, Eddie Whitcombe, Ron Stone, William Down.

Ottery St Mary Cricket Club, 1982. Left to right, back row: T. Fogwill, Jimmy Giles, Ken Clarke, S. Tabley, John Tierney, John Akers, D. Lambeth; front row: G. Cottle, John Ackroyd, Richard Whittington (captain), Tom Buckley, John Williams, Ray Pollard.

Ottery St Mary Cricket Club, 1998. Left to right, back row: *John Lovell (umpire), Andy Berry, Paul Hird, Mike Cox, Rob Johns, Richard Kitzinger, Rick Maloney, Terry Perryman (scorer);* front row: *Jonathan Wilson, David Culshaw, Barry Flicker (vice-captain), Richard Lock, James Perryman.*

of new members from Ottermill Switchgear. Matches were being played at the club's present ground at Salston Field off Strawberry Lane, to which it thought to have moved during the 1920s from Salston House itself. This ground was a school playing-field used by the King's School with the club having a licence to play a certain number of matches during term time and in the school holidays. However, in June 1969 the club was granted a 15-year lease of the ground and was able in January 1978 to acquire the freehold. The present clubhouse was then built and it was opened by Brian Rose, the Somerset and England cricketer, in April 1979.

Before the clubhouse was built members drank in various public houses in the town. At one time meetings were held in an upstairs room in the Volunteer Inn and the annual dinner was held at the London Hotel. The landlord of the London Hotel was for many years 'Curly' Coates, who was a member of the 'Handlebar Club' comprising mainly ex-RAF members who sported handlebar moustaches. This club played a cricket match against Ottery St Mary in 1953.

The cricket club has been fortunate in having many members who have served well both as players and in administrative capacities. One remembers John Morgan, captain for around five years and treasurer for even longer, Howard Scroll (now in New Zealand) and Graham Cottle (now Judge Cottle) and,

in more recent years Mark Woodman and John Tierney, both of whom played for the club in the 1980s and then moved to Exmouth, both playing for Devon on many occasions and appearing at Lords in the Minor Counties Cup final and gaining a winner's medal. In 2004 John Tierney is back with the Otters and proving an asset. One must mention past chairmen Richard Whittington and Barry Flicker who worked so hard for the club, as well as John Lovell the secretary in 2004 and, for many years, one of the club's umpires. Robert Bradshaw-Smith is the new chairman (from 2004), a position his father, Dr Jeremy Bradshaw-Smith, held in the 1970s. Robert is a fine batsman and a medium-fast bowler. It is thought that Robert holds the record for the club's highest individual score of 193 not out against a touring side when he won the match by scoring 26 in one over. On the bowling side Colin Marshall took all ten wickets for only ten runs in a 2nd XI league match against Exeter Civil Service 2nds in 1991.

Ottery St Mary has had an active junior section with at least 40 youngsters playing for county sides including Colin Perry, Charles Taylor and Alan Lovell. The old *Midweek Herald* Youth Cup was won on two occasions and the Devon U16 Cup semi-final reached on several occasions. The club is a member of Bradley's East Devon Youth Cricket League and in the last few years some age groups have won their league. Many junior members have moved on to play senior cricket – there are too many to mention but one thinks of Colin Perry, who went on to captain the club's 1st XI, and Tom Bornet and Mat Kirk who have won 1st XI trophies. This active junior section has helped the club to progress in many ways including obtaining funding for an all-weather wicket and other all-weather practise facilities.

The club has been fortunate to entertain sides from Somerset CCC on several occasions, staging benefit matches for such Somerset stalwarts as Hallam Moseley, Peter Denning, Brian Rose and Colin Dredge. The first time a side came from Somerset was in 1958 to celebrate the club's centenary. It is said that the meeting to select the team took several hours. The club captain for the day was Group Captain Laurie Spencer, OBE, and the team included Bryce 'Charlie' Lamb who was chairman for many years, and Harry Channon, a fine medium-fast bowler and middle-order batsman.

The match against Somerset that really stands out in the memory is that which followed the opening of the clubhouse when the county side, batting first, posted 355–5 with Ian Botham scoring 141 in just 60 minutes, hitting the balls onto the clubhouse roof and out of the ground. Frank Beer who took three of the wickets that fell finally bowled him. Even Tom Buckley, a mainstay of the club for years and a fine slow bowler and a good batsman, suffered at the hands of Ian Botham, although he did dismiss Phil Slocombe for 96. Tom was a local pharmacist and the club also had a local doctor, Jeremy Bradshaw-Smith, as a member and a local lady said she liked being looked after by Tom and Jerry. Returning to the Somerset match, Ottery were bowled out for just 38 runs with only John Lovell (9) and John Ackroyd (6) being the highest scorers – Ackroyd's six runs came off one ball. Ackroyd was also a doctor and he will remember more vividly a later Somerset match when he bowled out the West Indian Viv Richards for 27 runs.

Local people all remember 1968 as being the year of the big flood with several bridges being washed away, including one at Tipton St John. The cricket ground was under several feet of water with a caravan being washed onto the field from the adjoining site and the club tea house being pushed off its foundations; cricket was resumed after three weeks thanks to the hard work of club members.

The cricket club again attracted the headlines in the 1990s when a resident of the caravan park that runs cheek by jowl with the pavilion-side boundary became annoyed at the number of six hits that was landing on his mother's caravan. In a fit of temper he drove into the field and on to the square and refused to budge. Obviously, in due course, he was removed and curtly informed that cricketers had been hitting sixes into that field long before the caravans had been there.

During the 1970s, John Stone, a club member who had moved back to London, sponsored a team that played at Ottery St Mary for several years and on occasions Test and County players including John Price, Mike Smith, Clive Radley, Ron Hooker, Brian Gould and Mike Gatting visited the Salston ground. It was quite an experience to face John Price, an England opening bowler, and when Mike Gatting caught an Ottery batsman at slip he was heard to say that it saved him running down to third man.

In 1982 the East Devon Cricket League was formed with Ottery St Mary as one of its seven founding members, the other six being Alphington, Axminster, Bradninch, Countess Wear, Cullompton, London & Manchester, and Whimple & Whiteways, Honiton RBL being the eighth member a year later. The Ottery St Mary team was runner-up in the first season, won the league in 1983 and was runner-up again in the next three seasons (1984, 1985 and 1986). The 2nd XI were founder members of Division Two in 1984 when they won the title, a feat they repeated in 1986, following with second place in 1987 and 1998. In 2001 the East Devon League merged with the Devon league, Ottery St Mary playing in the D Division East. Ottery St Mary's league (either East Devon or Devon) records are as follows:

1st XI
Best Stands For Ottery St Mary

First	123 Martin Miller, John Williams v Axminster in 1991
Second	110 John Tierney, Barry Flicker v Yarcombe in 2003
Third	147 Mel Bligh, Robert Bradshaw-Smith v Chardstock in 1997
Fourth	166 Robert Bradshaw-Smith, Barry Flicker v Upottery in 1995
Fifth	132* Jimmy Giles, John Williams v Kentisbeare in 1988
Sixth	107 Nick Whitehead, John Tabley v Countess Wear in 1985
Seventh	67* Robert Johns, Ian Pugsley v Clyst Hydon in 2003
Eighth	88* Robert Bradshaw-Smith, Rick Maloney v Feniton in 1996
Ninth	78 Richard Lock, Mike Cox v Whimple in 1995
	78 David Guthrie, Mike Cox v Exeter South in 2000
Tenth	41 Charles Culshaw, Mike Mallett v Countess Wear in 1995

Best Stands Against Ottery St Mary

First	158 Adrian Codling, Stuart Bright for Feniton in 1995
Second	130 Roger Smith, Malcolm Paiva for Whimple in 1999
Third	132 Adrian Skirrow, Pete Skinner for

Countess Wear in 1995

Fourth   114 Phil Spong, Steve Reed for Axminster in 1990

Fifth   147 Barry Jarrett, John Causley for Exeter Civil Service in 1985

Sixth   105 Mat Kirk, Ian Pugsley for Culmstock in 2003

Seventh 88* Keith Hanford, Gary Vercoe for Countess Wear in 1993

Eighth   57 Charles Rendall, Peter Hurt Kentisbeare in 2003

Ninth   59 Mark Boswell, Gerry Carpanini for Honiton in 1990

Tenth   40 Andy Brinsford, Simon Persse for Honiton in 2003

Highest score for Ottery St Mary – 267–8 v Whimple in 2002

Highest score against Ottery St Mary – 324–7 by Upottery in 1995

Lowest score by Ottery St Mary – 32 v Whimple in 1991

Lowest score against Ottery St Mary – 52 by Whimple in 1986 and 52 by Exeter South in 2000

Highest innings for Ottery St Mary – 163 by Robert Bradshaw-Smith v Whimple in 2001

Highest innings against Ottery St Mary – 136 by Dave Carnall for Feniton in 1997*

Best bowling for Ottery St Mary – 8–35 by John Tierney v Whimple in 1986

Best bowling against Ottery St Mary – 8–21 by Mike Bright for Upottery in 1999

Most runs in a season – 610 by Robert Bradshaw Smith in 1995

Most wickets in a season – 50 by Jimmy Giles in 1987

2nd XI
Best Stands For Ottery St Mary 2nds

First   130 Richard Whittington, Richard Saunders v Uplyme in 1988

Second 142 Derek Hayward, Colin Berry v Clyst Hydon 2nds in 2000

Third   166 Andy Marks, Derek Hayward v Exeter South in 1991

Fourth   105 Mike Cox, Dave Richards v Yarcombe 2nds in 2002

Fifth   106 Robert Johns, Mike Clarke v Uplyme 2nds in 1995

Sixth   64 Richard Lock, Colin Marshall v All Saints in 1993

Seventh 57* Mike Cox, Mike Mallett v Yarcombe 2nds in 1997

Eighth   51 Keith Quaintence, Ben McEwen v Cullompton 2nds in 1995

Ninth   78* John Burnell, Mike Mallett v Yarcombe 2nds in 1999

Tenth   53 Dick Taylor, Richard Culshaw v Kentisbeare 2nds in 1995

Best Stands Against Ottery St Mary 2nds

First   222 Gary Kennard, Nigel Wyatt for Upottery in 1994

Second 128 R. Slade, Mike Blackmore for Halberton in 1985

Third   195 Tim Drake, Keith Baker for Sidmouth 3rds in 1997

Fourth   148* Andy Pengelly, Pete Reed for Tiverton in 1994

Fifth   117 Phil Spong, Ross Faverty for Axminster 3rds in 2001

Sixth   111 Nathan Groves, Dave Lapping for Honiton 2nds in 2000

Seventh 87 Steve Palfrey, Steve Carder for Whimple in 1990

Eighth   24 Dave Vallance, Nick Vallance for N St Cyres in 1996

Ninth   51* Geoff Herbert, Kevin Salter for Riverside in 1990

Tenth   53* Jeremy Reed, John Hall for Tiverton in 1989

Highest score by Ottery St Mary 2nds – 259–5 v Yarcombe 2nds in 2001

Highest score against Ottery St Mary 2nds – 296–8 by Kentisbeare 2nds in 1995

Lowest score by Ottery St Mary 2nds – 21 v Whimple 2nds in 1994

Lowest Score against Ottery St Mary 2nds – 23 by Exeter CS 2nds in 1991

Highest innings for Ottery St Mary 2nds – 126 by Derek Hayward v Yarcombe 2nds in 2001

Highest innings against Ottery St Mary 2nds – 124 Rehann Caryl for Exeter CS 2nds in 1997*

Best bowling for Ottery St Mary 2nds – 10–10 by Colin Marshall v Exeter CS 2nds in 1991

Best bowling against Ottery St Mary 2nds – 8–19 by Mike Barrett for BR (South) in 1988

Most runs in a season – 411 by Colin Atkinson in 1996

Most wickets in a season – 50 by Colin Marshall in 1991.

(* indicates an unbroken partnership or a not-out innings.)

Cricket has always been a game that is full of figures but there is more to it than that. And there is much more that can be said about Ottery St Mary Cricket Club and many more members named. The club has been part of the town's story for 146 years providing pleasure and leisure activities for men of all ages. May it continue to grow and be an asset to the town.

Ottery Rovers Cycling Club

Revd Kelly was certainly a firm believer in the Victorian concept of muscular Christianity. Besides being the president of the rugby club, he accepted an invitation to hold the same position to the Ottery

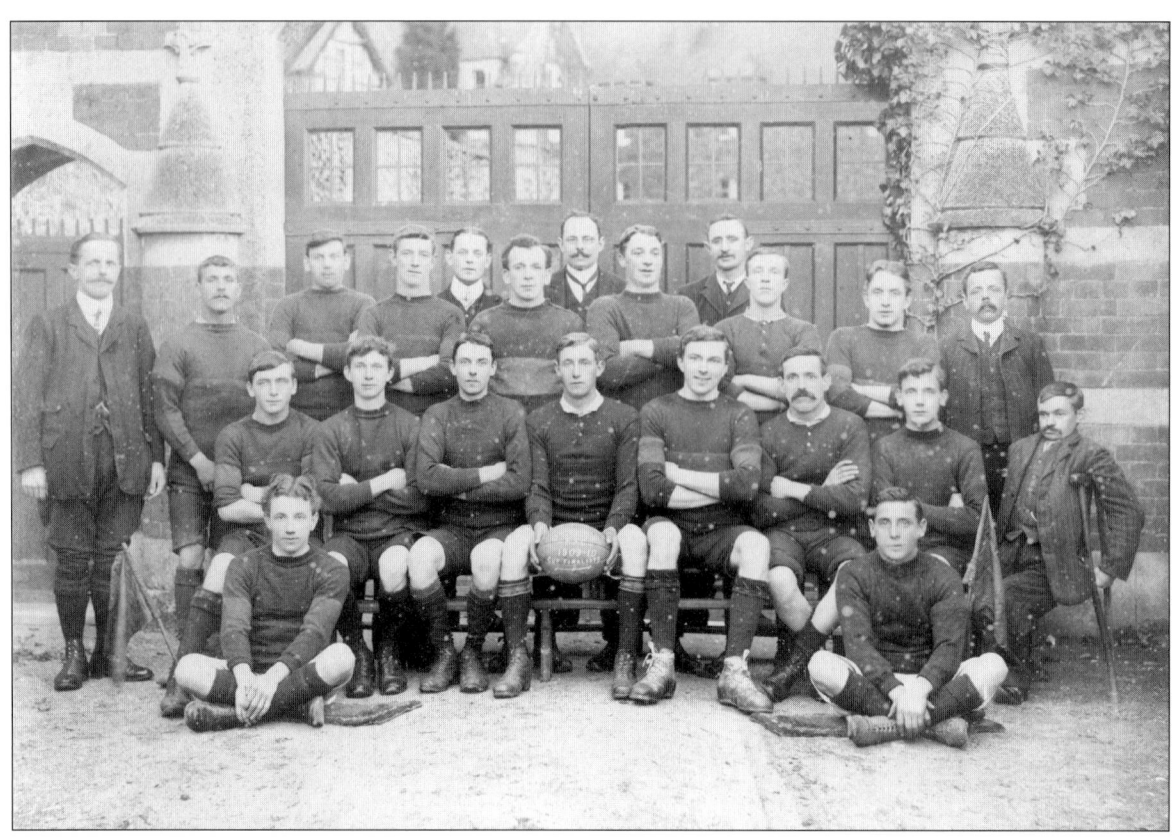

The Ottery St Mary Rugby Football Club at the end of the 1909/10 season, the year they were runners-up in the Devon Junior Cup.

Ottery St Mary Football Club, 1923/27, outside the entrance gate to the Chanter's House, a popular place for team photos at the time.

Rovers Cycling Club formed in 1895. He was supported by the captain, J.H. Mayer, and treasurer, W. Tucker. There were over 20 members and the new club's first run was to Tipton St John.

Ottery St Mary Rugby and Football Clubs

Ottery St Mary Rugby Club was formed in 1889 (it was called Ottery St Mary Football Club in the press at the time) and struggled to survive at first. So much so, in fact, that in 1894 a meeting was held in the Church House at which, in view of the declining membership, a proposal was made that the club should fold. However, the club continued and flourished for a while under an active committee that included Revd M. Kelly as president with F.E. Yole the chairman and R. Hore as captain.

Support dwindled once again and the club disbanded in 1911, with its funds totalling £3.0s.11d. (£3.05 in today's money) being transferred to the football club. The football club was formed at the final, poorly-attended AGM held by the rugby club in the Institute Hall on 29 August 1911, with the president, the Hon. Lord Coleridge, in the chair. There were very few rugby players present and a move was made to switch to the association code, but no decision was reached for either rugby or football and Lord Coleridge, obviously a rugby devotee, resigned. He then asked for nominations for a chairman, secretary,

treasurer and committee for the rugby club – none were forthcoming and the club was disbanded.

The following Saturday night, with Mr F. Wyatt, the headmaster of the King's School, in the chair, an association football club was formed. The officers elected were: chairman, Mr F. Wyatt; secretary, Mr A.F. Casley; treasurer, Mr G.H. Tobey; captain, Mr F.H. Street; vice-captain, Mr E. White; committee, Messrs R. Hake, Frank Luxton, A.H. Carnell, J.H. Melden, W. Pithers, C. Wagland, F.H. Stuckey and Paddon. It was decided to enter the East Devon Football League and the Football Express Cup.

The Otters played their first match on 30 September 1911, away to a Countess Wear side that started with nine men, although one more arrived soon after the start. Ottery won 4–0, Edwin Street, H. Stone and Pithers (2) scoring. Pithers was a centre-forward of some ability and had considerable senior experience with various Exeter clubs. The next game was at home to Otterton & Bicton United and this time the Otters won 3–0. No teams were given in press reports of Ottery's league games, the first such mention of a team being made in the report of their 2–1 win over Lyme Rovers in the semi-final of the Football Express Cup at Axminster when the Otters were: A. Street, F. Street, T. White, Luxton, Harrison, Titcombe, E. Street, Bowman, Pithers, Bastin and Down.

The choice of the Axminster ground (then at Gravelpit Field off Chard Road) for the semi-final may have been open to question. In an earlier round

Ottery St Mary Football Club, 1947/48. Left to right, back row: *Hector Stuckey, Lionel Heale, Jimmy James, Ivor Tucker, ? Griffiths, ? Woodley, ? Cleverton, R. Eveleigh, ? Reed;* middle row: *Maurice Baker, Derek Heale, Fred Piney, Fred Turner, R. Marks, Ron Codling;* front row: *Leo Dolling, Roy Isaac, John Bluck, Eric Manning, Jock Osborne.*

Ottery St Mary Football Club, c.1955. Left to right, back row: Fred Turner, Roland Lovering, Reg March, Len Russell, Derek Heale, David Cann; middle row: Derek Russell, Eric Manning, Digger Ebdon, Pete Spurway, J. Greenaway; front row: Tony Carter (mascot).

Ottery St Mary Football Club, 1933/34, the season they won the East Devon and Victory Football League Central Division and Divisional Cup. Left to right, back row: H.J. Westaway, Walter Eveleigh, H.J. Rew, Walter Hammett (president), E. White, Frank Richards, C.S. Purdy; middle row: Jack Woodley, Reg Eveleigh, I. Inglefield, Fred Ash, J. Ryell (captain), Lionel Heale; front row: Hector Stuckey, Albert Berry, Richard Ebdon, Fred Stuckey, Richard Eveleigh.

Ottery St Mary Football Club, 1951/52, with the Morrison Bell Cup and the Axminster Hospital Cup. They won the Hospital Cup, beating Perry Street League side Merriott 5–1 in the final at Axminster and, in the Morrison Bell Cup final, they beat Colyton 3–1. Left to right, back row: *Harry Griffiths, Gordon Russell, Reg Marks, Fred Turner, Donald Baker, Roland Lovering, Dave Cann, Ern Phillips;* front row: *Len Russell, Eric Manning, Derek Heale, Richard 'Digger' Ebdon, Peter Spurway, John Greenaway, D. Russell;* mascot: *Tony Carter.*

West Hill Football Club, 1920/21.

the Otters had startled the local footballing world by sensationally defeating the well-established Axminster Town club 4–3 at Ottery St Mary in the same competition. The Ottery St Mary correspondent's report in *Pulman's Weekly News* made no mention of the fact that Axminster had played with ten fit men for over an hour after their Sam Mitchell was injured and made only a token contribution on the wing. There was quite a bit of feeling during and after the game, Axminster protesting that there were no goal nets, the cross-bar was defective (they claimed this robbed them of two goals) and Ottery's centre-forward Pithers was a senior player. The protest was thrown out, the Ottery correspondent for *Pulman's Weekly News*, perhaps misguidedly, using the pseudonym 'Sportsman', gloating that:

Axminster were too cocksure of winning... it was not nice to see a team of Axminster's reputation take a defeat in such an unsportsmanlike manner... they continually barracked the referee who, on one occasion, took the flag away from their linesman and handed it to another member of the club.

Axminster did not take the remarks kindly and their answer the following week said that Ottery:

... being a new club were not accustomed to playing before a crowd who understood the rudiments of football... and it is therefore unfair of them to stigmatise those who appreciate the niceties of the game... with regard to barracking the referee, this is false [a euphemism for lying] *what can be said of supporters who barrack the visitors as they walk back through the public streets... commend the Otters to pluck the first mote.*

If it had been a contest to see who wrote the best report, Axminster would have won on style, sarcasm and use of the language spoken by Shakespeare. But the Otters had the last laugh – they had won the game even if Axminster won 5–2 in the same cup's first round at Ottery the following season.

The games were played on the same field that the rugby club had used beside the old Saw Mills and the Market Place but, if *The Golden Jubilee Book of Ottery St Mary (1887–2002)* is to be believed, a move would soon be made to the field beside St Saviour's Bridge where the modern bonfires are lit, the first of five homes the club played at between 1911 and around 1959.

All football clubs faced enormous problems in the seasons immediately following the Second World War when, via the County FAs, the FA warned that 'no concessions can be made for the supply of rationed goods'. This included football kit, which, like all other clothing was rationed until 1949. At that time everyone had 66 clothing coupons per year and, if you were a footballer, you needed 14 of them to go out on the field: five for your pair of boots, four for the shirt, three for the pair of stockings and two for the shorts. A goalkeeper's jersey could take as many as eight, but only five if it was not all wool. Clubs could apply for a grant of clothing coupons but were expected to find a reasonable (and unstated) amount themselves. The procedure was for each club to collect loose

Ottery St Mary Argyle Football Club, 1920/21.

coupons from their players and then to forward them to the Board of Trade who would exchange them for negotiable vouchers. A far more sensible method would have been for clubs to apply for an agreed amount per team through their County FA, but there were potential problems with the player who provided coupons for his shirt, and was then dropped for someone who had not. And even if you got a set of shirts you might not find any in your club's normal colours. Neighbouring Seaton were unable to get their white shirts and settled for the green and white ones they still play in at the time of writing. Beer Albion were luckier than most; someone gave them a set of shirts and, even if they were red and not in their traditional Oxford and Cambridge blue, they were not going to look a gift horse in the mouth.

The problems were not restricted to clothing. No permits were needed for goal nets, the manufacture of sporting nets being permitted, but getting your hands on a set was another matter and timber was in short supply if your goal posts had not survived the war.

Players were advised to take their own soap and towel with them and teams were also advised to take their own ball to away games for the pre-match 'kicking-in'. Before the war it had been the job of the home side to provide both teams with balls for this purpose, a sensible habit that the postwar shortages killed off.

With so many men arriving home at the last minute, either on leave or demobilisation, players were allowed to be signed-on by handing their registration form to the referee before the game instead of waiting seven days before being allowed to play. The Exeter & District (later Devon & Exeter) League, unlike the Perry Street League that was up and running for the 1945/46 season six weeks after the atom bomb was dropped on Hiroshima, waited until 1946/47 before it restarted.

After the Second World War a move was made to Shutes Mead at the foot of Chineway and for a short spell the club moved to another field off Slade Road – it would have been a very short spell (probably two seasons) because Beer Albion president Robbie Driver recalls playing in a Morrison Bell Cup final against Ottery St Mary at Shutes Mead in the 1958/59 season (he also remembers going as a small boy with Beer to the pitch in the bonfire field), and the club moved to its present home at Washbrook Meadows about two years later. Since then there has been considerable development at Washbrook Meadows, beginning with a clubhouse c.1974 that cost £8,000 and was replaced in 1990 by a bigger one at a cost of almost £40,000. Floodlighting was installed in 1986 and first used in a game with Division One side Queens Park Rangers that marked the opening.

The club played in the old East Devon & Victory League (later Exeter & District League), reaching the Premier Division after winning the championship of the Senior One Division in 1953/54. They struggled in the higher level, finishing bottom in 1955/56 but, because promotion and relegation were not automatic at the time, they stayed up and went down the following season only to be champions of Senior One again in 1961/62.

Since then they have steadily made progress joining the Great Mills League in time to be First Division champions in 1989/90 and gaining promotion to that league's Premier Division. Since then the club has lost some ground and in 2004 are competing in the Firewatch Devon League.

Between 1920 and 1960 the Morrison Bell Cup (given by local MP Sir Clive Morrison Bell) was the cup that East Devon sides most wanted to win. Ottery St Mary never won the cup, however, until the competition restarted after the Second World War in 1950. They made up for that lack of success by playing in an astonishing eight of the first ten postwar finals including the first five in a row. Those eight finals ended as follows: 1951/52 beat Colyton 3–1; 1952/53 lost 5–1 to Seaton Athletic; 1953/54 beat Rockbeare 8–1; 1954/55 lost 3–1 to Beer Albion; 1955/56 lost 3–2 to Beer Albion; 1957/58 lost 2–0 to Lympstone; 1959/60 lost 2–0 to Beer Albion; 1960/61 beat Lympstone 5–2.

Two members of the club warrant special mention. First is Richard 'Digger' Ebdon who left the club in 1935 to start a professional career with first Exeter City and then Torquay United. He is covered more fully in Chapter 13. There have been many other splendid players in the club, including one who went on to become one of the longest-serving officials in the history of the Devon & Exeter League. He is Eric Manning who started as a centre-forward after the Second World War, moved to left-back and (in 1963/64) actually played in all 11 positions including goalkeeper. He played until he was 40 and soon after hanging up his boots he became secretary of the league and in the 2003/04 season has held that post for some 36 years. And they have been 36 years of dedicated service that have earned him the respect and affection of all who have served with him.

The Ottery & District Football League

The Ottery & District Football League came into being after the First World War when there was considerable expansion in local football; one of the offshoots of this was the formation of a league open to clubs in that part of East Devon that is centred around Ottery St Mary.

A general meeting of clubs was held in the Volunteer Inn at Ottery St Mary on 1 March 1921 when Mr Reg Blackmore of the East Devon League presided over an attendance of around 40 people, including Mr A.J. Tidball, secretary of the East Devon

Jim and Rosemary Pearcy. Jim Pearcy, East Devon's 'Mr Football,' has given most of his life to the game that he loves and is still very actively connected with, and is a welcome visitor to any ground, in the area. An Escot man born and bred he played for the club for 20 years (1951–71), finally retiring after breaking a leg. He was a very good centre-forward (they call them strikers today), just how good can be seen from his feat of once scoring 18 goals in four games. His haul went seven in an 11–1 win against Otterton, five (Farway won 9–1), nil (Feniton lost 0–3) and six (Kentisbeare won 11–0). His playing career was interrupted by National Service in the Royal Air Force between 1954 and 1956. In 1960 he married Rosemary at Aylesbeare. His playing days over he began putting something back into the game that he had got so much pleasure from. He joined the committee of Escot Rovers in 1963, became vice-chairman in 1970 and was secretary from 1876 until 1981 when the club folded. He joined the Golesworthy Cup Competition committee and became chairman in the mid-1960s – a post he still holds in 2004. Between 1976 and 1978 he was an Area Independent member of the Devon FA and became a member of the Devon FA council in 1978. He was also Eastern Area vice-chairman (1984–2001), vice-chairman of the Devon FA (1988–89) and was made a life member of the Devon FA in March 1999. And Devon's highest football honour cannot been more deserved. Jim has another sporting love – skittles – which he still plays at the time of writing. His passion really started in 1960 when the Woodbury & District Skittle League was formed and he joined the Milers team, for whom he became treasurer in 1964 and is still in office in 2004. He joined the Woodbury League committee in 1967, was vice-chairman in 1970, chairman 1972, vice-president in 1988 and president in 1990 – another position he still occupies at the time of writing. Added to his many years of service to local sport is a warm-hearted personality, liked and respected by all who have ever met him. All in all a remarkable man.

League, and other officials. Among the clubs represented at the meeting were Newton Poppleford, West Hill United, Escot Rovers, Broadhembury, Sidmouth Scouts, Ottery St Mary Scouts, King's School (Ottery St Mary), Ottery Argyle and East Budleigh Argyle. The chairman remarked that the meeting was convened for the purpose of considering the question of a league to serve a radius of 12–14 miles of the town. Mr Tidball carefully outlined the rules of the East Devon League and, following a proposal of Mr Meldon (West Hill) that was seconded by Mr Cox (Newton Poppleford) a league was formed along the same lines as the East Devon League. Mr Meldon was the new league's first secretary with Mr W.T. James (Ottery St Mary) as chairman, with a Mr Casley of West Hill being elected as treasurer later. The first committee consisted of Mr E.W. Cox, Mr S. Clarke (Talaton), Mr Freddie Syres (Fairmile) and Mr F.J. Harris (Broadhembury). The MP for the Honiton constituency, Major Clive Morrison Bell, became the first president. The first list of vice-presidents almost reads like an Ottery St Mary and district hall of fame, including as it did, Lord Coleridge, Sir John Kennaway, Sir Ernest Satow, Lord Clinton, Cedric Drew (later Sir Cedric and Major Morrison Bell's successor as MP for the Honiton constituency) and Colonel Balfour.

Further meetings were held and the rules used by the East Devon League were adopted. That league also gave one of the spare trophies that they possessed for the new league to use as its championship trophy. The secretary told the committee that he had received an offer of a five-guinea (£5.25) challenge cup from the Ottery St Mary silversmith, Mr Arthur Golesworthy, for a cup to be competed for by the junior teams in the Ottery St Mary district. This competition is still known as the Golesworthy Cup and is still competed for in 2004 – 83 years later.

Recorded in the early minutes of meetings held is the name of the Escot Rovers secretary, John 'Jack' Ireland Selway, who became the league secretary from 1928 until the league became defunct in 1965. He continued to be the secretary of the Golesworthy Cup competition for some years after that.

The first team to fall foul of the new league's rules were the Ottery St Mary Boy Scouts who played an unregistered player against Escot Rovers during the first season. Today they would be fined heavily but, back then, only a vote of censure was passed. Escot Rovers themselves were the next to break a rule when they arrived 30 minutes late for a match at Sidmouth when their car broke down. They received no punishment this time, but when they were late at Otterton their excuse was that they were unable to find the ground and changing-rooms, and a fine was imposed. At the end of the first season the treasurer was able to report a balance of £1.3s.11d.

The league ran from 1921 until 1931 when there was a break for a season, after which it ran until 1938. It was restarted after the Second World War in 1946/47. The Golesworthy Cup was taken over by the league at that time.

Despite its trials and tribulations the Ottery & District Football League was always a friendly,

Escot Rovers Football Club, 1946/47, with the Axe Vale League champions trophy, the Ottery & District League trophy and the Divisional Cup. Left to right, back row: Bert Maher, Phil Pike, Jack Palfrey, Ern Mummery, Percy Skinner, George Hawkins, Dave Summers, Ern Taylor, Jack Selway; front row: Harold Lovering, Dolfuss Summers, Gerald Beer, Frank Bastin.

family affair and its matches were mainly conducted in the true spirit of the game – many players still remember with affection the days they spent playing in it and the many friends they made through doing so. The list of teams that have enjoyed that friendship is considerable, including as it does: Payhembury, Broadhembury, Newton Poppleford, Escot Rovers, Talaton United, Sidmouth Scouts, West Hill United, Otterton, Ottery St Mary Scouts (the nine founding fathers), Plymtree, Sidbury, Alfington, Weston, Clyst Hydon, Whimple, 4th Devons, Ottery Town Reserves, Honiton Territorials, Budleigh Salterton, Rockbeare, Farrington House, Aylesbeare, East Budleigh, Tipton St John, Woodbury Argyle, Beer Albion Reserves, Awliscombe, Southleigh Rovers, Feniton, Upottery, Dalwood, Netherton United (Farway), Branscombe, Colyton, Offwell (later Offwell & Widworthy), Honiton British Legion, Axmouth United, Gittisham, Farway, Kentisbeare, Honiton Town, Clyst Rovers, Kilmington, Willand Rovers, Exmouth Town Colts, Seaton Town Reserves, Topsham Town Reserves and Uffculme – 48 in all. Some made fleeting appearances – Uffculme played for just one season – and others, such as Escot Rovers, played in every season that the league ran.

Life Members
Mr J.H. Meldon (1937)
Mr A.J. Casley (1946)

Presidents
Major Arthur Morrison Bell MP   *1921–31*

Sir Cedric Drewe	*1932–45*
Sir John Kennaway	*1946*
Dr Sidebottom	*1947–49*
Colonel G. Morse	*1950–65*

Chairmen
W.T. James	*1921–29*
A.E. Golesworthy	*1930–65*

Secretaries
Mr J.H. Meldon	*1921*
Mr S.J. Gollop	*1922–24*
Mr J.H. Meldon and Mr E.W. Cox	*1924*
Mr J.I. Selway	*1925–65*

Treasurers
Mr A.J. Casley	*1921–45*
Mr P.G. Blackmore	*1946–65*

Ottery & District League Champions
1921/22 Otterton
1922/23 Otterton
1923/24 Sidmouth
1924/25 Rockbeare
1925/26 Rockbeare
1926/27 Woodbury
1927/28 Payhembury
1928/29 Ottery St Mary
1929/30 Clyst Hydon
1930/31 Clyst Hydon
1931/32 No competition

The Escot Rovers football team that lost 2–1 to Sidmouth in 1953/54. Left to right, back row: Terry Lovering, Frank Bastin, Percy Skinner, Len Salter, Alec Bright, Philip Pike; front row: Francis Blackmore, Arthur Wright, Jim Pearcy, Sailor Brown, John Welsh.

1932/33 Dalwood
1933/34 Dalwood
1934/35 Talaton
1935/36 Broadhembury
1936/37 Broadhembury
1937/38 Broadhembury
1938/46 No competition
1946/47 Escot Rovers
1947/48 Newton Poppleford
1948/49 Otterton
1949/50 Otterton
1950/51 Otterton
1951/52 Kentisbeare
1952/53 Feniton
1953/54 Gittisham
1954/55 Gittisham
1955/56 Gittisham
1956/57 Gittisham
1957/58 Gittisham
1958/59 Gittisham
1959/60 Farway
1960/61 Farway
1961/62 Ottery St Mary

Morrison Bell Cup

Major Arthur Morrison Bell MP presented the Morrison Bell Cup for a knockout competition between amateur football clubs in the Major's Honiton (later East Devon) constituency. In later years professional players were permitted to play and, following the boundary alterations to the East Devon constituency, teams that were formerly in the constituency were still invited to play. At the time of writing, Budleigh Salterton have won the cup on 17 occasions, followed by Sidmouth Town (10) and Ottery St Mary (8).

Morrison Bell Cup Winners
1919/20 Axminster Town
1920/21 Exmouth Church Institute
1921/22 Beer Albion
1922/23 Axminster Town
1923/24 Exmouth Church Institute*/Beer Albion*
1924/25 Colyton
1925/26 Seaton
1926/27 Beer Albion
1927/28 Sidmouth Town
1928/29 Withycombe
1929/30 Budleigh Salterton
1930/31 Sidmouth Town
1931/32 Beer Albion
1932/33 Budleigh Salterton
1933/34 Exmouth Town
1934/35 Budleigh Salterton
1935/36 Lympstone

1936/37 Lympstone
1937/38 Exmouth Town
1938/39 Lympstone
1940/50 No competition
1951/52 Ottery St Mary
1952/53 Seaton Athletic
1953/54 Ottery St Mary
1954/55 Beer Albion
1955/56 Beer Albion
1956/57 Exmouth Town
1957/58 Lympstone
1958/59 Lympstone
1959/60 Ottery St Mary
1960/61 Beer Albion
1961/62 Budleigh Salterton
1962/63 Ottery St Mary
1963/64 Sidmouth Town
1964/65 Ottery St Mary
1965/66 No name listed
1966/67 Sidmouth Town
1967/68 Budleigh Salterton
1968/69 Budleigh Salterton
1969/70 Sidmouth Town
1970/71 Exmouth Town
1971/72 Sidmouth Town
1972/73 Ottery St Mary
1973/74 Sidmouth Town
1974/75 Sidmouth Town
1975/76 Sidmouth Town
1976/77 Budleigh Salterton
1977/78 Ottery St Mary
1978/79 Sidmouth Town
1979/80 Honiton Town
1980/81 Clyst Valley
1981/82 Budleigh Salterton
1982/83 Exmouth Town
1983/84 Budleigh Salterton
1984/85 Budleigh Salterton
1985/86 Honiton Town
1986/87 Budleigh Salterton
1987/88 Ottery St Mary
1988/89 Exmouth Amateurs
1989/90 Exmouth Town
1990/91 Budleigh Salterton
1991/92 Exmouth Town
1992/93 Budleigh Salterton
1993/94 Feniton
1994/95 Budleigh Salterton
1995/96 Culm United
1996/97 Budleigh Salterton
1997/98 Exmouth Amateurs
1998/99 Budleigh Salterton
1999/00 Budleigh Salterton
2000/01 No competition (foot-and-mouth epidemic)
2001/02 Cullompton

joint holders

Chapter 11

The King's School

Bishop Grandisson chose Ottery St Mary as the site at which he would found his college that, he said, was 'to provide a sanctuary for piety and learning.' The college was formally inaugurated at Christmas 1337, the rebuilding of the church being finished five years later in 1342. The population of the college consisted of 40 members, eight canons, eight vicars choral, eight junior clerics, eight choirboys and eight other members, including a chaplain who also acted as the choirmaster, a parish priest and a schoolmaster. Grandisson is thought to have given the college the astronomical clock now in the church – one of only three or four similar medieval clocks in the country, others including those in Exeter and Wells Cathedrals. By 1445 there was a chained library with books numbering 150, many of them bequeathed to the college by Grandisson himself. Besides the library, the college buildings included a chapter house and a schoolhouse with buildings providing accommodation for the college members.

Around two centuries later the college fell victim to the dissolution of the monasteries, when it surrendered to Henry VIII's commissioners in 1545 and its contents were plundered or destroyed. The Henrican iconoclasts also destroyed many of the buildings in order to use the building stone and roofing lead, quite a bit of which went towards the rebuilding of Cadhay House. The church itself survived as Parish Church.

The college school was founded as the 'Kinge's Newe Grammar Scole' by Henry VIII, but to say that Henry founded the school is something of a misnomer. It would be more accurate to say that he refounded it, and even that is open to argument, because there was a perfectly good college already in existence and it had been so for almost exactly two centuries.

The college's status in its heyday is shown by the visits paid to it by Henry VI in 1452 and Henry VII in 1497. Its net annual income from the manorial lands amounted to £300 (say £100,000 at least in today's money). Henry VIII's commissioners' inventory survives and shows the college to have had over 300 ounces of silver vessels, 200 books and innumerable richly embroidered copes and other vestments that were normally worn by priests in procession.

The King's School, Ottery St Mary, c.1925.

The workforce that built the King's School at Ottery St Mary in 1911 pose for their picture before the laying of the foundation-stone. The elderly, white-bearded gentleman (below) is Sir John Kennaway.

The King's School hockey team in 1915. The long skirts must have slowed the game up considerably.

The King's School tennis team in 1915.

The old Ottery King's School, 1880. It was closed in 1883 under a scheme of the Charity Commissioners and the site and buildings were sold. It was demolished in 1884.

Pupils head from Ottery King's School towards the station (in the case of Honiton and Sidmouth pupils) and the town around 1950.

Despite the King's School becoming moribund in the early-nineteenth century, it recovered and still continues to the time of writing as a very successful King's School. At first the school was located in the Priory, where it restarted in 1894.

Overcrowding, a problem with many such schools at that time, led to the school moving to larger purpose-built premises at Thorn on the Exeter Road on 23 January 1912. John Whitham in his book Ottery St Mary tells us that 'with this move, the King's School became the first co-educational in Devon.' Its neighbour at Colyton followed it in this respect when girls were first admitted there on 6 May 1913. However, Colyton Grammar School must be the claimant to be the first grammar school in Devon, if not in England, to have appointed a headmistress, Mrs Susannah Stokes having occupied that post between 1772–75.

Ottery King's School under-15 cricket team in 1960.

An aerial view of the King's School at Ottery St Mary in the 1960s.

Other Schools

The Girls' School, Ottery St Mary, June 1953. Left to right, back row: *Margaret Lovering, Jennifer Luxton, Mrs Newton (teacher), Pamela Baker, Betty Parsons*; middle row: *Mary Dyer, Doreen Knight, Lynda Blackmore, Celia Heywood*; front row: *Marion Stanford, Hilary Carn.*

Ottery St Mary Boys' School, 1948.

Ottery St Mary Boys' School, c.1934. Left to right, back row: F. Turner, A. Gigg, Viv Verschoren, B. Johns, Frank Down, L. Salter, Miss Hooper; third row: ?, R. Gibbons, Derek Heale, N. Drew, Archie Retter, Tony Cann, P. Arbury, Joel Wonnacott, J. Ayres; second row: G. Sparkes, Jeff Woodley, F. Bending, J. Palfrey, S. Willis, O. Taylor, G. Whitwell; front row: R. Luxton, ?, J. Retter, K. Hawkins, Mick Avery, Brice Bending, A. Isaac, E. Palfrey.

Ottery St Mary Boys' School, 1932–33. Left to right, back row: ?, Gerald Retter, Steve Wheaton, Clive Retter, John Franks, Don Hadfield, Bill Johns, Viv Verschoren, Miss Hooper; third row: Don Dyer, ? Pike, Reg Shapter, Wilf Baker, ? Palfrey, Stan Bolt, ? Palfrey, Derek Heal, Grenville Matthews; second row: Archie Retter, Stanley Young, George Urquhart, Peter Arbury; front row: Brice Bending, Tony Cann, Tommy Tolman, Jeff Woodley, Mick Avery.

Ottery Boys' School football team, 1932/33. Left to right, back row: Mr Rogers, Reg Marks, Don Palfrey, G. Small, Ern Temple, Mr Bowden; middle row: Wilf Woodley, Alf Wheaton, Fred Piney, Jim Gapper, Les Dolling; front row: Cyril Dyer, Les Andrews, Fred Davey, Bob Knight, Maurice Thorne.

Chapter 12

Utilities

The Post Office

In the eighteenth and early-nineteenth centuries Ottery St Mary had a sub-Post Office rather than a Post Office in its own right, with the mail being brought from Honiton where the London–Salisbury–Blandford–Dorchester–Axminster–Honiton–Exeter mail coach called daily. The Ottery St Mary mail was brought out to the town and delivered by a foot postman, and later a mail cart was used. The foot post collected any mail that had been handed in at the local sub–Post Office. Although the Royal Mail ran its coach from Axminster on to Exeter via Honiton, by the closing years of the eighteenth century there was also a horse post to Exeter that went via Colyton, Sidmouth, Budleigh, Exmouth and Topsham, and some Ottery St Mary post from those towns could possibly have been unloaded at Sidmouth and sent by another foot post.

Since the eighteenth century there had been a charge of one penny to cover the cost of the journey to the Post Office and the letter was usually, but not always, hand-stamped to show that the penny had

been paid. Not unnaturally the system was called the Honiton Penny Post. It was not unique to Honiton – almost every small town that had a Post Office served its smaller neighbours and, thus, there was an Axminster Penny Post, a Bridport Penny Post, an Exmouth Penny Post and so on. Many people confuse the Penny Post with the universal postal system introduced in May 1840 because of the Penny Black stamp that was introduced in May of that year – certainly until at least 1998 *The New Oxford Dictionary of English* did so. Sir Rowland Hill's new postal arrangement did not herald in a universal penny charge on letters, only on the first weight step; heavy letters cost more, as the introduction of the world's second postage stamp, the Two Penny Blue, a few days after the Penny Black, indicates.

Ottery St Mary's mail reached or left Honiton by four different types of posts – London letters, country letters, cross-post letters and bye-letters. The first group is self explanatory, letters that went direct to or from the capital. Country letters passed through London on their way to their final destination, say Honiton to Norwich. As the name suggests, a

The Post Office's 1974 Christmas set depicted bosses from various churches throughout the country. The eight-penny value depicts the Blessed Virgin and Child; it is the last but one to the west of the roof at Ottery St Mary's Parish Church.

The Post Office in Mill Street, Ottery St Mary, c.1910.

The Post Office staff at Ottery St Mary, c.1908.

The Ottery St Mary 'squared-circle' postmark in use from the 1880s until the early years of the twentieth century (in some towns until the early 1920s), the cds (circular date stamp) that replaced it and the cds used by the receiving house (later a sub-Post Office) at Fairmile. The fourth postmark is an unusually late (28.12.1903) usage of the Duplex mark that was replaced by the 'squared circle'. It was probably found in the back of a drawer or kept in case the 'squared-circle' hand stamp was lost and it was used until a replacement was received.

cross-post was one that went 'across country' and did not touch London on its way from one provincial town to another, e.g. Honiton, Taunton, Bristol, Cardiff and many others. Bye-letters travelled along the main coach runs without getting as far as London, from Honiton, say, to Salisbury or Andover. Once the letter arrived at Honiton from the receiving houses, the number of miles it had to travel decided the cost of conveying it to its final destination. Before the introduction of the Universal Penny Post and the postage stamp the charges were considerable, although the rate tended to be lowered for longer distances. Thus, although a letter from Honiton to Yeovil cost about six pence, one to London cost only about 11 pence.

Receiving houses were found in a variety of places. Ottery St Mary's was in Mill Street, almost certainly where the Post Office is in 2004. It was certainly there in 1841 but others in East Devon could be found in a grocer's shop (Beer), a baker and stationer (Branscombe), a boot- and shoemaker (Colyford), a lace manufacturer (Colyton – where, later, the headmaster of Colyton Grammar School had a licence to sell stamps at the school when it was in the Church House in the centre of the town), a wheelwright (Chardstock), a schoolmaster and librarian (Rousdon and Combpyne), three successive shoemakers (Farway) and, best of all from the point of view of the foot post who covered the villages, an inn at Luppitt and at Kilmington where John Chapple, a sub-postmaster was also the landlord of the Old Inn.

In 1857, when John Joseph Reed was the postmaster, the London mail arrived (via Honiton) at 6.30a.m., from Sidmouth at 8.32a.m. and again at 6.45p.m., and from the North at 5.45p.m. Rural deliveries were being made to Tipton St John, Harpford, Payhembury and Venn Ottery, Newton Poppleford, Colaton Raleigh and Larkbeare at 7.00a.m., having arrived in Ottery St Mary at 5.30a.m. The first wall box in the town was outside the Post Office; it was last emptied daily at 6.30p.m. except on Sundays.

The universal penny post introduced by Sir Rowland Hill on 5 May 1840 may not be accepted as

one of the great reforming social benefits of the nineteenth century, but it should be. By considerably reducing the cost of the postage to be paid, Sir Rowland had put keeping in touch with one's family within the reach of even the humblest classes and the number of letters carried by the Post Office trebled almost overnight and increased annually throughout the Victorian era. This was true of Ottery St Mary where around 100,000 items were being sent by 1846.

Some people had enjoyed a 'free post' prior to the arrival of the postage stamp when it was the recipient of the letter, rather than the sender, that actually paid the postage that was due. Many a parent with a son or daughter working away from home often adopted a code that a regular letter from their children meant that they were in good health and the parent refused to accept the letter, which was permissible at the time. The arrival of the postage stamp put an end to that, but it opened up another way to cheat the Post Office when the stamps were floated off their covers (envelopes) and, for obvious reasons, the black postmarks were not easily seen on the black stamps. At first the postmarks were changed to red and, when that was not always satisfactory, the Penny Black was printed in red and not unnaturally is universally known in the philatelic world as the Penny Red – the longest-serving stamp in British postal history (from 1841–87).

The Railway

Although the railway reached Exeter from Waterloo in 1860 there was a 14-year wait before the 'Iron Horse' reached Ottery St Mary when the Sidmouth branch line was opened on 6 July 1874. Besides Ottery St Mary the only other station along the branch line was at Tipton St John. The new line ran from a main-line station called Feniton Road, because of its proximity to the village. Its name was changed to Sidmouth Junction after the branch line was closed. It was renamed Feniton Station many years later.

On 15 May 1897 another line was opened from

Ottery St Mary Railway Station, c.1910. The crowd is waiting for the train that is to take them for a day at the seaside at either Sidmouth or Exmouth.

Ottery St Mary Railway Station seen just before its closure in 1967.

Ottery St Mary Railway Station, c.1906, with would-be passengers waiting for the Sidmouth Junction train as it approaches the platform. The line was closed in 1967.

The old goods shed at Ottery St Mary's station was run by Miller and Lilley, the Honiton-based corn and coal merchants. Later, and after the station was closed, Ottery St Mary Saw Mills took over, but the business closed and the buildings were demolished to make room for newer businesses on the Finnemore Industrial Estate.

Ottery St Mary Railway Station.

The signal-box at Ottery St Mary station shortly before it closed in 1967. When the station was built in 1874 the signal-box was on the other side of the line. Inside, the station looks deserted (below) – one of the reasons that it was closed, along with the entire Sidmouth branch line, by the Beeching report.

The Tuck Shop was originally a railway carriage and placed outside the railway station, a strategic position to capture the trade of pupils heading towards the King's School.

Tipton St John to Budleigh Salterton with stops at Newton Poppleford, Colaton Raleigh and Otterton on the way. In 1903 it was extended to Exmouth and that made it possible to catch a train direct to Exmouth, a trip that became very popular in the summer and for school trips.

The run to Sidmouth, especially through Harpford Woods in the spring, was also popular, and quite a feat of engineering to climb the lower slopes of East Hill, along the bottom of which the River Otter winds in a large 'S' bend. The East Hill ridge rises to 700ft at Bulverton and 750ft at Fire Beacon. At Tipton St John you could see the Sidmouth line rising steeply to the left, a gradient accentuated by the fact that the Exmouth line was seen running downhill, the two lines running side-by-side for a short distance. On 6 March 1967 Dr Beeching closed the line and all the station buildings, except Sidmouth Junction, of course, have vanished or have been converted into houses.

Other Utilities

The second half of the nineteenth century saw a considerable increase in the benefits available to the inhabitants of the town. The water-supply was brought into the town in 1852, the Town Hall opened in 1860, the town was lit by gas for the first time in 1865, and the cottage hospital was opened in 1870. There was an electric telegraph available in the Post Office by 1871 and the telephone put in an appearance in the very first years of the new century. The gas-lit street lamps were made redundant by blackout regulations during the Second World War and although the sturdy posts survived, albeit in a rather rusty condition, their delicate burners and other working parts rusted away and electricity soon took over.

The telephone exchange in Jesu Street, Ottery St Mary, in 1962. Left to right: ?, Janet Collins, ?, Marion Paddon (behind), Pat Harris, Margaret Hadfield.

Chapter 13
❖
Ottery St Mary Worthies

THE R.T HON. SIR JOHN H. KENNAWAY, B.T. C.B., M.P.
FATHER OF THE HOUSE OF COMMONS

THE CHANTER'S HOUSE.

THE R.T HON. SIR ERNEST M. SATOW, G.C.M.G. REPRESENTATIVE OF THE BRITISH EMPIRE AT THE HAGUE PEACE CONFERENCE.

THREE OTTREGIAN WORTHIES

ESCOT HOUSE

THE LORD COLERIDGE. JUDGE OF THE HIGH COURT OF JUSTICE

BEAUMONT HOUSE

Alexander Barclay

Although it is not known for sure if Alexander Barclay was born in Scotland c.1475, we do know that for a spell he was a secular priest at Ottery St Mary, where he was appointed as chaplain of the college in 1509. Later he became a Benedictine monk until the dissolution of the order in 1538. Entrusted with the spiritual education of Princess Mary (later Mary I) as her household chaplain, he deserted her in 1551 and, under the influence of Archbishop Cranmer in the reign of Edward VI (1547–53), he became a Protestant. His death in 1552 allowed him to escape the fate of Cranmer when he was burnt at the stake during the Marian persecutions.

Alexander Barclay translated Sebastian Brant's early-sixteenth-century satiric *Book of Fools* into English. During his time as a Benedictine monk he wrote English eclogues or pastoral poems and also made various translations from Italian and Latin.

John Billiatt

John Billiatt was the longest-surviving member of the Stuart expedition, the first to cross Australia in 1861–62. There were 12 members of the expedition when it left Melbourne in 1861, most of them under 21 years of age. Billiatt only got in because Stuart had thrown out another member due to insubordination. They were faced with a 2,000-mile journey across some of the most inhospitable land in the world.

The entry in Billiatt's diary for the day before the start of the expedition reads 'my wardrobe consisted of three Crimean shirts, two pairs of boots, one necktie and two pairs of trousers.' It took nine months to make the crossing and, when they reached the northern coast the party hoisted the Union Flag. Long before the end, Stuart was so close to death that he had to be carried in a stretcher made from the skin of a horse that had been shot, partly because of the lack of fodder, and partly to save Stuart's life. Billiatt also helped Stuart by making a jelly from that horse's tongue and lips for him.

Billiatt himself was not in too bad a shape, even if the wear and tear of the crossing had led to his trousers, which he took back to England with him as a souvenir, having as many as 39 patches on them. But he left behind him his name for all time; there is still a Billiatt's Spring in North Australia and, at the spot where the historic journey was completed, a Stuart's Point. Stuart never really recovered from the hardships he had encountered and died in London just five years later (1866).

John Billiatt married his sweetheart, Ann Elizabeth King, but he was not finished with adventure and, in 1872, with his wife and two young daughters joined an expedition to Paraguay. Its intention was to raise cattle and export meat to Great Britain but the venture was not a success and the Billiatts were back in South Australia in 1875 in Glenelg, a seaside town named after a small west-coast village in Scotland. The Billiatt family finally returned to England when John's mother was taken ill. He moved to West Hill in 1896 where he built a house for his family and sisters. It was called Wurlie, after the octagonal tents used by Stuart's men, and contained many unusual features linked with the expedition. Sadly, perhaps, in 2004 it is called Elsdon. Ann died in 1905, Billiatt remarrying and moving to Exeter.

In 1912 the South Australian Government decided to mark the fiftieth anniversary of the raising of the Union Flag on the northern Australian coast by presenting the surviving members of the expedition with a gold watch each. Billiatt received his in Exeter from the hands of the then Premier of South Australia, Hon. A.H. Peake.

The last survivor of the expedition, Billiatt died in 1919 and was buried at St Michael's Church at West Hill. On the gravestone can be found the words, 'The last survivor of Stuart's expedition, the first to cross Australia 1861–62.' After his death his daughters returned to Adelaide with the remaining relics of the expedition.

In 2002 Billiatt's grave was restored, thanks to generous donations from the members of the Stuart Society of South Australia and the Ottery St Mary Heritage Society.

Samuel Taylor Coleridge

There can be little argument that Samuel Taylor was the most worthy of Ottery St Mary's worthies. He was certainly the most famous, and not just for his 'Rhyme of the Ancient Mariner'. He wrote many more fine works about his native town and the river from which it takes its name, although the later works are probably much less known to the world:

As late I'd o'er the extensive plain
Where native Otter sports his scanty stream,

Musing in torpid woe a Sister's pain,
The glorious prospect woke me from the dream,

At every step it widen'd to my sight –
Wood, Meadow, verdant Hill and dreary Steep,
Following in quick succession of delight,
Til all – at once – did my eye ravish'd sweep!

(Life, 1789)

And, four years later:

Dear native Brook! Wild streamlet of the West!
How many various fated years have past,
What happy and what mournful hours, since last
I skimmed the smooth thin stone along the breast,
Numbering its light leaps! Yet so deep imprest
Sink the sweet scenes of childhood, that mine eyes
I never shut amid the sunny ray,
But straight with all their tints thy waters rise,
Thy crossing plank, they marge with willows grey,
And bedded sand that veined with various dyes
Gleamed through thy bight transparence!

(Song of the Pixies, 1793)

He alludes to St Mary's Church with:

... I dreamt
Of my sweet birth-place, and the old church-tower
Whose bells, the poor man's only music, rang
From morn to evening, all the hot Fair-day,
So sweetly, that they stirred and haunted me
With a wild pleasure, falling on mine ear
Most like articulate sounds of things to come!

(Frost at Midnight, 1798)

Samuel Taylor Coleridge (1772–1834) from a 1795 painting by Van Dyke.

Samuel Taylor Coleridge was born at the School House in Ottery St Mary on 21 October 1772. He was the tenth child, and ninth and last son of the vicar of Ottery St Mary, the Revd John Coleridge and his second wife, Anne Bowden. There were four daughters by an earlier marriage but contact between the half-brothers and sisters seems to have been minimal at the very best. The baptismal entry in St Mary's Church register reads: '1772, Dec. 30. Samuel Taylor, son of John and Ann Coleridge, the Vicar, born Oct. 21st last at about eleven o'clock in the forenoon'. Coleridge's father could well be included in a list of the town's worthies – the King's School being well known for its high standards during his time there. Sadly, for the Coleridge family as well as the King's School, Coleridge senior died on 4 October 1781 when the poet to be was but nine years of age.

Samuel Taylor Coleridge's education started at the age of three when he attended a dame-school, from where in 1778, at the age of six, he left to become a pupil at Ottery King's School where he was an above-average pupil, although unsuited to become a clergyman, a calling that his father, not unnaturally, hoped he would follow. His father was unable to put any pressure on his son because he died when Samuel was young and Mrs Coleridge and her large family were forced to leave the School House to make way for the new vicar. They took up residence in the Warden's House and, despite the shortage of money, she was able to find a place for her youngest son to be educated with other poor children in London at Christ's Hospital. Samuel's closest friend was Charles Lamb whose parents took pity on the lonely boy. Lamb mentions Ottery St Mary in his tragedy 'John Woodvil' ('Those are the sweet bells of Ottery St Mary... my native village... in the sweet shire of Devon') although it is highly unlikely that he ever visited Coleridge's home town himself.

He went to Jesus College, Cambridge, but in a state of near poverty, after an attempt to raise cash through a lottery ticket misfired when he did not win anything, he joined the King's Regiment of Light Dragoons under a false name. He was soon uncovered and discharged and he resumed his education at Cambridge.

Coleridge married Sarah Fricker, the sister of the poet Robert Southey's wife, on 4 October 1795 at the Church of St Mary, Bristol and they set up house at Clevedon. He had fallen out with his brother George but was reconciled with him and the rest of the family when he took Sarah to meet them at Ottery St Mary.

With his wife he had a son, Thomas Hartley Coleridge, who became a poet in his own right, as did his son Ernest Hartley Coleridge who, writing of the cottage at Nether Stowey where the couple settled, said:

Stranger, beneath this roof in bygone days
Dwelt Coleridge. Here he sang his witching lays
Of that Strange Marine, and what befel
In mystic hour, the Lady Christabel
And here, what time the summer's breeze blew free,
Came Lamb, the gentle-hearted child of glee;
Here Wordsworth came, and wild-eyed Dorothy!

The unveiling of the blue plaque in 2000 by Richard Holmes, Coleridge's biographer, on a wall to commemorate the birth of Samuel Taylor Coleridge on 21 October 1772. He was born in the Vicar's House, which is thought to have been in the vicinity of the wall. The plaque was a gift from the Ottery St Mary Heritage Society.

Richard 'Digger' Ebdon

Probably the toughest centre-forward ever to play for Exeter City, Digger Ebdon was born at Ottery St Mary on 3 May 1913. He joined Exeter City as a professional in 1935 after a few games for them as an amateur. He was the old-fashioned centre-forward going in where it hurt without the slightest hint of fear, a style that brought him 51 goals in 144 games for Exeter despite the fact that the Second World War cut five years out of his career. In 1948 he joined the 'old enemy', Torquay United, and after retiring as a professional he played for his native Ottery in the Exeter District League when over 40 years of age, helping them to win the Senior One championship in 1953–54 and promotion to the Premier Division. A much-respected man, he died on 27 April 1987.

William Makepeace Thackeray

Although William Makepeace Thackeray's connection with Ottery St Mary is more tenuous than that of Samuel Taylor Coleridge, he most certainly is worthy of being a worthy (sorry) of the town. His early career was that of a journalist and he was rendered almost penniless when, at the age of 22, the money his father had left him was lost in the Indian bank failure of 1833. He would write for both *Punch* and *Fraser's Magazine*, but it is probably fair to say that of all his works, *Vanity Fair*, published in serial form between 1847–48, is the most remembered if not the best.

Other works included *The Book of Snobs* and the *Newcomers* and, in his later years, he was the founding editor of the *Cornhill Magazine*.

Thackeray spent most of his school holidays with his stepfather at Larkbeare near Fairmile and the happy times he spent in and around Ottery St Mary provided him with the background for his 1848 novel Pendennis, in which Ottery St Mary is scantily disguised as Clavering St Mary, the birthplace of the novel's autonomous hero Arthur Pendennis, and the River Otter becomes the River Brawl. If it had not already been done, the game was given away in the first edition of the novel that included a vignette of St Mary's north tower.

Thackeray died in 1863 aged 52.

Sir Ernest Satow, GCMG, Hon. LLD (Camb), DCL Oxon.

Sir Ernest Satow was born on 30 June 1843 and for 23 years was a member HBM Consular Service in Japan, followed by spells as HBM Minister at Bangkok, Montevideo, Tangier and Tokyo and Peking. He retired to Ottery St Mary where he died on 26 August 1929 when the parish magazine gave him the following tribute:

Richard 'Digger' Ebdon in the early 1950s after his professional career with Exeter City and Torquay had ended and he had rejoined his native Ottery St Mary club.

It was indeed at Nether Stowey that Samuel would write some of his best poems including the 'Rhyme of the Ancient Mariner'. Nether Stowey is roughly halfway between Bridgwater and Watchet on the A39 and in 2004 the cottage is in the hands of the National Trust and well worth a visit.

But debt, and probably the addiction to opium that Coleridge acquired, contributed to the separation of the poet and his wife. This caused a rift between Samuel and his brothers, especially George, and, although there was reconciliation, he never visited Ottery St Mary again.

Ottery St Mary's greatest son died on 25 July 1834 at Highgate Village, aged 61, and was buried in the local cemetery. His friends, the Gillmans, had a tablet placed in the church in his memory. On it he was described as a poet, philosopher, theologian and, 'This truly great and good man'. Few would argue with the latter sentiment.

A very full account of his work as a dimplomatist [sic] in various countries was given in the Times and other newspapers. But that was only one part of a many-sided character... he seldom spoke of the great work that he had done and of the many countries that he knew so well, although he was officially consulted until quite recently. Japanese statesmen were reported to have said when they were asked a question about the customs of Japan, 'If you want to know anything about Japan or its customs, you had better ask Satow.' Sir Ernest was a great linguist... one of his last tasks was to read the Bible through in Russian that he had taught himself late in life. Besides being always in his place at Matins, he was a regular and devout communicant to within a year of his death, when he became too infirm to come to church.

For many years he organised the assistant-curate's fund, and as a member of CEM, he was anxious that laymen should take an active interest in the church life of the parish. He was a generous and systematic supporter of the church funds and even up to the Sunday before his death sent his envelope for the Free Will Offering and his Sunday collection.

He was deeply interested in church schools and was disappointed that he was not co-opted to the Devon Education Committee before the War, when he had visited a large number of schools and made notes about them. The cause of the church overseas was very near his heart, and at one time he used to speak on their behalf. Strong, able, quiet, he was a great Englishman and a humble Christian.

A Miscellany

The East Devon Foxhounds at Salston House, Ottery St Mary on the occasion of the visit of Prince and Princess Alexander of Teck in 1905.

Threshing at Salston Farm, Ottery St Mary, c.1923.

Knightstone Manor, Ottery St Mary in 1906.

*Gosford House, Ottery St Mary. In the 1950s it was the home of Colonel Morse, the chairman of the Ottery &
District Football League.*

The fancy-dress parade during an unknown event in Ottery St Mary during the 1950s.

A 1920s Ottery St Mary outing to Cheddar Gorge stops and poses outside the entrance to the Cheddar New Stalactite Cave. Charabancs at the time were restricted to 12mph; if the speed limit was strictly obeyed this meant that the journey from Ottery took the best part of five hours – on rough and ready roads.

Mr M.P. Stuckey, an Ottregian in London, brought the first bicycle to Ottery St Mary in 1869. He is seen here on it outside the Boys' School in Yonder Street. He built the wooden machine and locals marvelled at the speed with which he drove down Tip Hill on it.

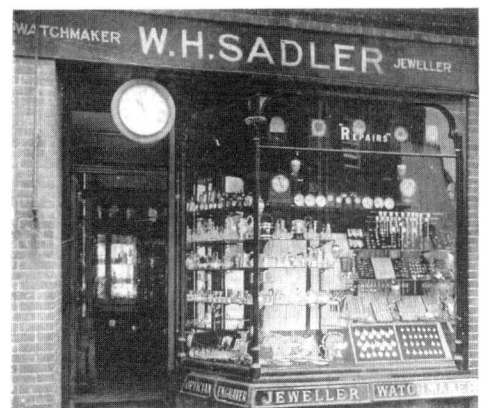

The Ottery St Mary Dance Band (the N.R.R.O.) in the 1930s. Left to right: ?, Alex Townsend, Fred Baker, Ern Selley, ?, Jim Crawford.

A lace class in Ottery St Mary at the Vicarage, c.1938. Left to right: Mrs Young, Miss Hines, Mrs Lee, Mrs Stallard, Mrs Lovell. The teacher, Mrs Whitcombe, is at the rear.

Ottery St Mary Sunbeam Juvenile Templars, the junior branch of the Independent Order of Grand Templars, taken in the gardens of Cornhill House, c.1910.

Alderman J. Malins, the Grand Chief Templar, leaving Broad Street after visiting Ottery St Mary during his national farewell trip to say goodbye to the various branches on his retirement, c.1910.

The Fatstock Show officials and judges pose behind the prizes. Lord Coleridge, the president, is on Lady Coleridge's right.

An Ottery St Mary charabanc outing to Gough's Cave, Cheddar. Judging by the solid tyres the picture has to date from around 1919.

Mr Inglefield presenting Nurse Loosemore with a TV set to mark her retirement.

Ottery St Mary's St John Ambulance Brigade, c.1963. Left to right, back row: Mrs Horton, Mrs Ash, June Shere, Mrs Hane, Rosemary Berry, ?, Mary Sergeant; second row: Molly Temple, Mrs Luxton, Margery Brewer, Dulcie Perry, Vera Hawke, Ruth Shere, Miss Turner; front row: Mrs McClymont, Mrs Denning, Sister Copping, Mrs Duke.

George Turner's butcher's delivery van, a bull-nose Morris, c.1930. He ran his business in Mill Street and did his own deliveries.

Ottery St Mary's St John Ambulance Brigade in the 1950s. Left to right: *Noel Oke, Harold Phillips, ?, Richard Eveleigh, Eric Parsons, Colin Turner.*

Ottery St Mary Congregational Church Sunday School outing to Harpford Woods on 11 August 1920.

The workforce of F.J. Luxton in the 1950s. He was an Ottery builder whose son Stuart runs the business from his yard in Tip Hill in 2004. Left to right: John Podbury, Alec Abbott, ?, ? Baker, 'Patchy' Piney, ?, Frank Richards, Bob Wood, Bob Pike; seated: Harold Phillips, ?, ?

Ploughing at Straight Gate Farm, Ottery St Mary, c.1914.

The Kings Arms Children's Christmas Party, c.1957. Among those present are: *Jenny Carter, Martin Coombes, Pete Mayne, Jenny Wills, Janet Keitch, Michael Luxton, Monty Perry, David Baker and Jennifer Bull.*

Regulars at the Lamb and Flag in Batts Lane take time off from the serious business of drinking to have their picture taken, c.1958. Left to right: Ted Bastyn (landlord), Reg Dyer, Reg Wheaton, Albert Hellier, Tom Willis, Tom Bull, Roger Potter, Harry Moore (in front), Fido Piney, Mr Salter, George 'Jago' Wellsman, Len Russell, Ernie Howe.

Mr and Mrs Northcott's wedding group at Ottery St Mary, c.1900.

Ottery St Mary Girl Guides, c.1925.

The Ottery St Mary Folk Dancers, 1926. Seventh from the left is Miss Sweetland who lived at Thorn Farm. Cis Manley, on the extreme right, ran a newsagents' business in Silver Street.

Firing the rock cannons in 1957. Left to right: Alex Abbott, Eddie Whitcombe, Leslie Salter, Peter Bull, Jim Isaac, Harry Channon, Nelson Owen, John Martin, Tony Bastin, Jim Pearcy.

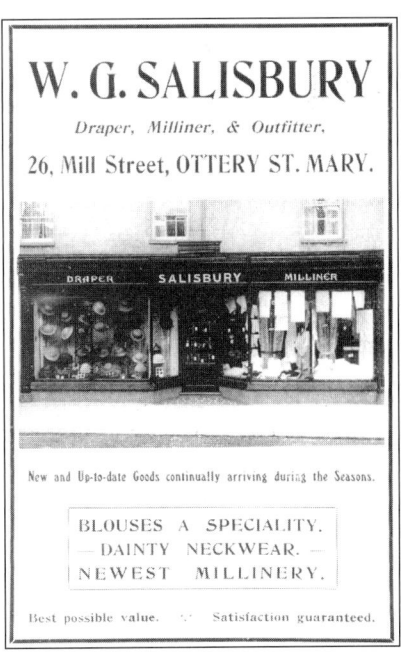

Ray Baker, Ottery St Mary's last town crier, in his ceremonial robes in 1992.

Bibliography

Coleridge, Hon. Phillis, *A Short Sketch of the Life of Samuel Taylor Coleridge*, Vail & Co, London, 1934.

Cornish, Sidney W., *Short Notes on the Church and Parish of Ottery St Mary*, Eland Brothers (revised), Exeter.

Eyre and Spottiswood Ltd, *Endowed Charities of Devon (Parish of Ottery St Mary)*, for His Majesty's Stationery Office, London, 1909.

Golesworthy, Maurice, Dykes, Garth, and Wilson, Alex, *Exeter City, A Complete Record, 1904–1990*, Butler & Tanner, Frome and London, 1990.

Griffiths, Arthur, *Ottery St Mary Urban District Council Jottings*, 1973.

Ottery St Mary Heritage Society, *The Golden Jubilee Book of Ottery St Mary*, Brightsea Ltd, Exeter, 2002.

Rose-Troup, Frances, *The Great Fire of Ottery St Mary*, James Townsend & Sons, Exeter, 1936.

Whitham, John A., *Ottery St Mary*, Phillimore & Co. Ltd, Chichester, 1984.

Whitham, John A., *The Church of St Mary of Ottery*, British Publishing Company, Gloucester, 1956.

Wreyford, Paul, *A Literary Tour of Devon*, Swift Print, Dawlish, 1996.

Subscribers

Antony C. Abbott, Ottery St Mary, Devon
Betty D. Abbott, Ottery St Mary, Devon
Vivien J. Arthur, West Hill
Tom H. Ash, Sidmouth, Devon
Don and Janet Baker, Ottery St Mary
Frances Bessie Baker, Ridgeway, Ottery St Mary
Joan Betty Baker, Ridgeway, Ottery St Mary
Mrs Betty Bastyan, Ottery St Mary, Devon
Jonathan and Catherine Battell, Ottery St Mary, Devon
Mr and Mrs J. Bird, Ottery St Mary, Devon
Mr and Mrs R. Bird, Honiton, Devon
Keith A. Bowden
Dr Jeremy Bradshaw-Smith, Ottery St Mary
S. Brewer, Courtfield House, Ottery St Mary
Alan T. Bright, Fairmile, Ottery St Mary
Charlie A. Broderick, Ottery St Mary, Devon
K.J. Burrow, Bucks Cross, Devon
Jennifer Cartwright, West Hill, Ottery St Mary, Devon
Michael and Janet Coombes, St Mary's Park, Ottery St Mary
Mary and Ken Corver, Taunton, Somerset
Carrie Crawford, Ottery St Mary
Dr Andy P. Davey, Guildford, Surrey
Michael Paul Diment, Ditton, Kent
Mr John and Mrs Beryl Donovan
Mrs Glad Down
Frank Down, Ottery St Mary
Mrs Jane Down
Ian J. Drake, Wiggaton, Ottery St Mary
Wendy E. Durling
Roger G. Evans, Tipton St John, Devon
Syd Foster
Mrs Marian Golesworthy
S.A. and P.K. Hamilton
K.G. Hansford, Ottery St Mary, Devon
John and Sylvia Harris, Ottery St Mary
Robert Harris, Bristol
Rosaline Helyer, Ottery St Mary
Brenda Hemmings, Ottery St Mary, Devon
Sam Hemmings, Ottery St Mary, Devon

The Holdens of Higher Metcombe
Mrs A. James, Ottery St Mary, Devon
Peter J. Jones, Ottery St Mary, Devon
Mr Stephen F. Jones, Ottery St Mary, Devon
Sheila M. Lawrence, Ottery St Mary, Devon
Katharine Lewis, West Hill
Sarah Lewis, West Hill
Myra Madge (née Tucker)
Dr Gerald and Mrs Rosalind Manley, Southerton, Ottery St Mary
Carol Marsh (née Crawford)
Mr and Mrs R.J. Mitchell, Ottery St Mary
Robert and Margaret Neal, Ottery St Mary, Devon
Dorothy Newson, Ottery St Mary, Devon
John and Marian Paddon, Ottery St Mary, Devon
Martin and Jenny Patterson (Seasons), Ottery St Mary
Mr Bert Pearcy, Cardiff, Glamorgan
Frank Perkins
Edie Pike, Escot, Ottery St Mary, Devon
Jeff Rowland, Ottery St Mary
Mr Leslie H. Salter, Budleigh Salterton, Devon
Richard J. Shaw, Ottery St Mary, Devon
William and Mary Shears (née Tucker), Wells
Frank Shepperd, Brixham
Stella Shepperd O'Leary, Chippenham, Wiltshire
Roger Smallshaw, Nailsea, Bristol
D. Stevens
Christopher and Pamela Stirling
Ralph H.G. Streat
Annie L.A. Taylor, Ottery St Mary, Devon
Ted, Lily and Peter Tozer, Ottery St Mary
Derek and Joy Turner, Ottery St Mary
Ronnie Urquhart, Twickenham
Peter and Valerie Venner, Ottery St Mary
D.W. Wakefield, Ottery St Mary, Devon
Clare Walker
John F.W. Walling, Newton Abbot, Devon
Mrs R.M. Webber, Ottery St Mary
Jennice L. Willis, Ottery St Mary, Devon
Glenda R. Woodley, Sunnylands Cottage, Ottery St Mary, Devon
Steven John Woodley, Sunnylands Cottage, Ottery St Mary, Devon
Peter A.H. Wyatt, Sidmouth, Devon

Community Histories

~◦~

The Book of Addiscombe • Canning and Clyde Road
Residents Association and Friends
The Book of Addiscombe, Vol. II • Canning and Clyde Road
Residents Association and Friends
The Book of Axminster with Kilmington • Les Berry
and Gerald Gosling
The Book of Bampton • Caroline Seward
The Book of Barnstaple • Avril Stone
The Book of Barnstaple, Vol. II • Avril Stone
The Book of Beccles • Pam Hardman and
Maureen Saunders
The Book of The Bedwyns • Bedwyn History Society
The Book of Bickington • Stuart Hands
The Book of Boscastle • Rod & Anne Knight
Blandford Forum: A Millennium Portrait • Blandford Forum
Town Council
The Book of Bramford • Bramford Local History Group
The Book of Breage & Germoe • Stephen Polglase
The Book of Bridestowe • D. Richard Cann
The Book of Bridport • Rodney Legg
The Book of Brixham • Frank Pearce
The Book of Buckfastleigh • Sandra Coleman
The Book of Buckland Monachorum & Yelverton •
Pauline Hamilton-Leggett
The Book of Carharrack • Carharrack Old
Cornwall Society
The Book of Carshalton • Stella Wilks and
Gordon Rookledge
The Parish Book of Cerne Abbas • Vivian and
Patricia Vale
The Book of Chagford • Iain Rice
The Book of Chapel-en-le-Frith • Mike Smith
*The Book of Chittlehamholt with
Warkleigh & Satterleigh* • Richard Lethbridge
The Book of Chittlehampton • Various
The Book of Colney Heath • Bryan Lilley
The Book of Constantine • Moore and Trethowan
The Book of Cornwood and Lutton • Compiled by the
People of the Parish
The Book of Creech St Michael • June Small
The Book of Cullompton • Compiled by the
People of the Parish
The Book of Dawlish • Frank Pearce
The Book of Dulverton, Brushford,

Bury & Exebridge • Dulverton and
District Civic Society
The Book of Dunster • Hilary Binding
The Book of Edale • Gordon Miller
The Ellacombe Book • Sydney R. Langmead
The Book of Exmouth • W.H. Pascoe
The Book of Grampound with Creed • Bane and Oliver
The Book of Hayling Island & Langstone • Peter Rogers
The Book of Helston • Jenkin with Carter
The Book of Hemyock • Clist and Dracott
The Book of Herne Hill • Patricia Jenkyns
The Book of Hethersett • Hethersett Society
Research Group
The Book of High Bickington • Avril Stone
The Book of Ilsington • Dick Wills
The Book of Kingskerswell • Carsewella
Local History Group
The Book of Lamerton • Ann Cole and Friends
Lanner, A Cornish Mining Parish • Sharron
Schwartz and Roger Parker
The Book of Leigh & Bransford • Malcolm Scott
The Book of Litcham with Lexham & Mileham • Litcham
Historical and Amenity Society
The Book of Loddiswell • Loddiswell Parish History Group
The New Book of Lostwithiel • Barbara Fraser
The Book of Lulworth • Rodney Legg
The Book of Lustleigh • Joe Crowdy
The Book of Lyme Regis • Rodney Legg
The Book of Manaton • Compiled by the
People of the Parish
The Book of Markyate • Markyate Local History Society
The Book of Mawnan • Mawnan Local History Group
The Book of Meavy • Pauline Hemery
The Book of Minehead with Alcombe • Binding and Stevens
The Book of Morchard Bishop • Jeff Kingaby
The Book of Newdigate • John Callcut
The Book of Nidderdale • Nidderdale Museum Society
The Book of Northlew with Ashbury • Northlew
History Group
The Book of North Newton • J.C. and K.C. Robins
The Book of North Tawton • Baker, Hoare and Shields
The Book of Nynehead • Nynehead & District
History Society
The Book of Okehampton • Roy and Ursula Radford
The Book of Paignton • Frank Pearce
The Book of Penge, Anerley & Crystal Palace •
Peter Abbott

For details of any of the above titles or if you are interested in writing your own history, please contact: Commissioning Editor, Community Histories, Halsgrove House, Lower Moor Way, Tiverton, Devon EX16 6SS, England; E-mail: katyc@halsgrove.com

In order to include as many historical photographs as possible in this volume, a printed index is not included. However, the Devon titles in the Community History Series are indexed by Genuki.

For further information and indexes to various volumes in the series, please visit: http://www.cs.ncl.ac.uk/genuki/DEV/indexingproject.html